JOY OF LIVING BIBLE STUDIES

DISCOVERING GOD'S PROMISES
Studies in Genesis 18–31

Practical Studies for Personal Growth

DORIS W. GREIG

Regal Books

A Division of GL Publications
Ventura, California, U.S.A.

Published by Regal Books
A Division of GL Publications
Ventura, California 93006
Printed in U.S.A.

Library of Congress Cataloging-in-Publication Data

Greig, Doris W., 1926-
   Discovering God's promises : studies in Genesis 18-31 : life-related for personal and group study / by Doris W. Greig.
      p. cm. — (Joy of living Bible study series)
   ISBN 0-8307-1361-1
   1. Bible. O.T. Genesis XVIII-XXXI—Study. 2. Women—Religious life. I. Title. II. Series.
BS1235.5.G742   1989
222'.11'0076—dc20   89-38119
                                                                              CIP

1 2 3 4 5 6 7 8 9 10 / 91 90 89

Rights for publishing this book in other languages are contracted by Gospel Literature International (GLINT) foundation. GLINT also provides technical help for the adaptation, translation, and publishing of Bible study resources and books in scores of languages worldwide. For further information, contact GLINT, Post Office Box 488, Rosemead, California, 91770, U.S.A., or the publisher.

CONTENTS

HOW TO GET THE MOST FROM THIS BOOK

The Bible is a living book! It is relevant and powerful, but more than that, it is the active voice of our living God, and He wants to communicate with you daily through His Word. As you study the Bible, you will learn about God's person and character. You will begin to find His purpose for your life as He speaks to you through His written Word. His purpose is unchanging and His principles are unfailing guidelines for living. He will show us His truth and what our response should be to it.

Will you set aside a special time each day to interact with God in His Word? As you read, study, meditate and memorize His Word, the Holy Spirit will guide you, and His direction for your life will be made clear. More and more, His voice will be easily discerned in the din of life's pressures. When your heart is available and you see God's good intentions for you, you will then learn how to respond to the Lord's personal call to you day by day, moment by moment. As you train your ears to hear the voice of God, you will recognize His presence in the most unlikely circumstances and places. "The grass withers and the flowers fall, but the word of our God stands forever" (Isaiah 40:8, *NIV*).

Try to have several versions of the Bible available as you study. Comparing these versions will enrich your understanding of a passage and bring added insight. Try not to use a commentary or any other reference work until you have allowed the Lord to speak personally to you through His Word.

Each lesson begins with a section of *Study Notes*. After Lesson 1, the introductory lesson, these Notes suggest ways to understand the passage at hand and relate it to other biblical teaching. Following the *Study Notes* is a section of *Questions,* designed to guide your Bible study through a six-day week. On the first day you review the pre-

5

vious Notes. And Days 2-6 will prepare you for the next lesson. You will benefit most from your study if you will do each day's questions at a regular time.

This study is designed to be used individually or in a group. If you are studying in a group, we urge you to actively share your answers and thoughts. In sharing we give encouragement to others and learn from one another.

This book has been conveniently hole-punched and perforated for easy tearout and insertion in a 6″ × 9½″ looseleaf notebook:

- Bible study pages lie flat in your notebook for ease of writing as you study.

- Additional notebook paper can be inserted for journaling or more extensive notes and other relevant information.

- Additional studies in the Joy of Living Series can be inserted, along with your personal notes, and tabbed to help you build your Bible study file for easy, future reference.

May God bless you as you begin your journey into His Word. This may be the first time for you to take this trip, or it may be that you have journeyed this way many times before. No matter what trip it is for you, we pray you will find new joy and hope as you seek to live in the light of the living God!

INTRODUCTION TO GENESIS

Study Notes

Genesis portrays Jesus Christ, our Creator, God. The word "genesis" came into the English language by way of Latin from the Greek. Genesis means "origin, or source, or beginning." This name was given to the first book of the Bible when it was translated into the Greek in the third century B.C.

All Our Beginnings Are in God

Genesis is the book of beginnings. *It gives the account of the beginning of all that the Creator brought into being.* Genesis answers our questions concerning the origin of the world, and of plant, animal and human life.

Genesis also records the beginning of a particular race of people, the Jewish people, who would safeguard this revelation by recording the holy Word of God as the Spirit of God led them. "For no prophecy recorded in Scripture was ever thought up by the prophet himself. It was the Holy Spirit within these godly men who gave them true messages from God" (2 Peter 1:20-21).

Genesis could be called the book of beginnings, for it records for us the beginning of the world, man, sin, civilization, nations, agriculture, machinery, music and poetry. It tells us of the world's first marriage, the first child born, the first murder committed, the first drunkenness, the first kingdom established and the first heathen temple. But the most wonderful thing that Genesis records for us is the beginning of God's work toward man and the promise of His Son, the Lord Jesus Christ, to us. Genesis reveals God's plans and purposes in His dealings with men.

7

We Meet the Divine
and Human Authors of Genesis

The author of the original book of Genesis is not known. It is safe to say that Moses by inspiration of the Holy Spirit is the final coordinating author of the book. However, the main part of Genesis occurred before Moses' life on earth, and therefore may originally have been written in different sections or repeated verbally from generation to generation until the time of Moses. Moses, by the inspiration of the Holy Spirit, put together into one book the story of Genesis for us, as God led him to write. Moses was prepared to understand the records, manuscripts and oral narratives by his training in "wisdom of the Egyptians" (Acts 7:22). He was a prophet who was granted the great privilege of unhurried hours of communion with God on Sinai (Exodus 19:3; 24:18; 34:2).

Obviously the men who first recorded the story of Creation fully believed that they were indeed recording the truth of God's creating power. The Bible tells us that God talked with Adam and Eve in the Garden of Eden (Genesis 2:16,17). God possibly told them the story of the Creation of the universe in a way that they could easily understand while they were in the Garden of Eden.

Some Bible scholars suggest that the unknown past of the Creation was revealed to the original writer of these chapters by a vision, just as John the Apostle wrote the last book of the Bible, Revelation, by a vision that was revealed to him (Revelation 1:19). Since there were no eye witnesses to God's creation, the first chapters of Genesis are a direct communication of God to someone. We need not be disturbed by the conflict of so-called scientific discoveries, but rather we are content to realize that eventually even science will have to come into agreement with the Word of God, which is forever settled in the heavens.

Let us never forget the importance of the phrase "In the beginning God created" (Genesis 1:1). *Around the Word of God is the protection of the Holy Spirit of God who inspired its words.*

Who wrote or told the Creation story used by Moses? Possibly it was written long before by Abraham, Noah or Enoch. Who knows? Writing was in common use before the day of Abraham. In Ur, Abraham's early home, as in every important city in Babylonia, there were libraries with thousands of books, dictionaries, grammars, reference works, encyclopedias, works on mathematics, astrology, geography, religion and politics.

Possibly Abraham had received traditions or records from Shem about the story of Creation, of the fall of man and of the flood. Abraham lived in a society of culture, books, and libraries. He probably

8

made careful and accurate copies of all that happened to him and of the promises that God had made to him. He put it down on clay tablets in the cuneiform writing to be handed down in the annals of the nation he was founding.

Thus Genesis records for us the beginning of everything except God. Without Genesis our knowledge of a creating God would be pitifully limited; we would be ignorant of the beginnings of our universe.

We Find Jesus in Genesis

Jesus Christ is the center of the Bible. He is somewhere on every page. In Genesis we see Him in type and prophecy in:

1. seed of the woman—Genesis 3:15
2. skins of slain beasts—Genesis 3:21
3. Abel's blood sacrifice necessary—Genesis 4:4
4. entrance into the ark of safety—Genesis 7:1,7
5. offering up of Isaac—Genesis 22
6. Joseph lifted from the pit to the throne—Genesis 37:28; 41:41-44

Redemption Planned, Prepared and Promised

That the two main parts of the Bible are referred to as the Old Testament and New Testament is not without reason. The word "testament" comes from the Latin *testamentum* or "covenant with God." In other words, the Old and New Testaments are records of the covenants between God and man.

When we understand that a covenant is a sealed agreement or promise between two parties, we are awed and humbled that almighty God should deign to covenant with mere man. And yet He has chosen to do just that through the many specific promises which He has given to us and which are recorded for us in God's Word, the Bible.

As we saw in our study of Genesis 1-17, the core of God's promises is redemption—our redemption—which He planned and prepared for us from the very beginning of time. We saw the first of these promises in the Adamic Covenant of Genesis 3:15 when God vowed that the seed (Jesus) of a woman would one day bruise the head of the serpent. In Genesis 9:9-17, we read of God's covenant with Noah, the rainbow becoming the sign of this covenant or promise that never again would He destroy the earth with a flood.

Subsequently, Genesis records God's covenant relationship with Abraham in which God called Abraham and promised to bless him and to make his name great. God also vowed that from Abraham's seed He would raise up a nation that would become the means by which redemption would come to bless not only the people of that nation Israel, but also those of all the Gentile nations on earth. These promises to Abraham were first given in Genesis 12:1-3 and renewed to him in 13:14-17; 15:1-14; 17:1-21 and—as we shall see in this study—again in 22:16-18.

The Promise of the Redemptive Nation

Why was this promise of becoming a redemptive nation given to Abraham? And why to his descendants?

As one scholar has noted:

> Two thousand or more years after the first hint of a Redeemer, the story of God's redeeming love enters upon a new phase. The ancient promise, amplified and repeated to many generations, was now to be implemented by the calling into existence of a *redemptive nation*, a nation absolutely unique in its origin, history, and mission, a nation whose privilege and responsibility it would be to bring the Christ into the world. Nothing is clearer in the development of this nation than that a God of love intended to give his all to win erring humanity to himself.[1]

So Abraham and his descendants became that redemptive nation, a free people of God's own choosing. And thus it was that God made His covenant with Abraham before he came to Canaan and renewed it when Abraham had arrived in his new land of promise. Because he believed God's promise, Abraham acted in obedience. Isaac and Jacob—whom we will also study in this unit—along with their descendants became heirs and custodians of the promise of redemption through faith.

Claiming the Promises of God

Our study of Genesis clearly shows that Abraham and his heirs were, like us, a self-willed and blemished people. They sinned, they gave into temptation and fear, and they frequently crumbled in the face of adversity. But as we also learn from them, God's promises are not conditioned upon man's worthiness, but rather upon God's faithfulness. And "he is faithful that promised" (Heb. 11:23).

Nevertheless, we cannot claim any of God's promises without faith on our part. We have already learned that Abraham, despite his

10

obvious humanity, was a man of faith. Repeatedly in Hebrews 11, we read of Abraham and others: "By faith Abraham," "By faith Isaac," "By faith Jacob," "By faith . . . ," "By faith . . . . "

"These all died in faith, not having received the promises, but having seen them afar off" (Heb. 11:13). Like them, we also must realize that "without faith it is impossible to please him: for he that cometh to God must believe that he is" (11:6).

Yes, God made a promise, but Abraham, by faith, claimed it for himself. And Abraham's faith in God's promise redeemed him. "Even as Abraham believed God, and it was accounted to him for righteousness" (Gal. 3:6).

> Individual salvation in Old Testament times was on the basis of faith's response to the promise made to Adam, later re-affirmed in the Abrahamic covenant . . . . Never has any man been saved in any other way than by faith either in the Promised Redeemer or in the Redeemer who has already come.[2]

Have you by faith claimed God's promise of salvation and redemption through Christ for yourself? In other words, have you claimed His promise of forgiveneses for your sins? If you have, then for you the covenant of promise has become the covenant of realization. If you have not yet put your faith in Jesus Christ as Lord and Savior, consider this promise from God's Word given to you:

> That if you confess with your mouth, "Jesus is Lord," and believe in your heart that God raised him from the dead, you will be saved. For it is with the heart that you believe and are justified, and it is with your mouth that you confess and are saved (Rom. 10:9-10).

As we now look in depth at Genesis 18-31 and study the faith journeys of Abraham, Isaac, and Jacob, let us discover together the many promises of God given to them and to us which are contained in these chapters. And let us ask God in prayer to write these promises on our hearts. May He also enable us by His Spirit to claim them, by faith, for ourselves.

Notes
1. Russell Bradley Jones, *A Survey of Old and New Testaments: The Bible Story of Redeeming Love* (Grand Rapids, MI: Baker Book House, 1957), p.55.
2. Ibid., p. 62.

Study Questions

Before you begin your study this week:

1. Pray and ask God to speak to you through His Holy Spirit each day.
2. Use only your Bible for your answers.
3. Write your answers and the verses you have used.
4. Challenge questions are for those who have the time and wish to do them.
5. Personal questions are to be shared with your study group only if you wish to share.
6. As you study look for a verse to memorize this week. Write it down, carry it with you, tack it to your bulletin board, tape it to the dashboard of your car. Make a real effort to learn the verse and its reference.

FIRST DAY: Read all of the notes and look up all of the Scriptures.

1. What was a helpful or new thought from the introduction to Genesis?

2. What was the most meaningful Scripture from the notes to you personally?

3. (Personal) Have you chosen to take up the challenge to give daily time to this study and to God? What sacrifice has God shown you that you could make to give time to Him in study and prayer? (Share if possible with your group, as it may help someone else.)

SECOND DAY: Read all of Genesis 18, concentrating on verses 1-8.

1. Where was Abraham's tent and who came to visit him there?

2. How did Abraham show his hospitality to strangers? Give verses.

3 a. Where did Abraham and Sarah feed their guests?

b. (Personal) Do you ever feel insecure about the food you have on hand or the condition of your home or apartment when an unexpected guest arrives? What lesson could a person learn from Abraham's hospitality?

4. Christians are to be hospitable. The Bible tells us this in many places. Put the following verses concerning hospitality into your own words.

Titus 1:7,8

Hebrews 13:2

1 Peter 4:9

5. (Personal) Are you hospitable to strangers? Do you invite others besides close friends to your home? Are you hospitable to those who are not hospitable to you—without grudging? Do you need to pray about this right now?

13

6 a. Challenge: Read James 2:18-26 and explain in your own words how it relates to Abraham's "works" of hospitality.

b. (Personal) As a Christian, are you as eager to have daily fellowship with the Lord as Abraham was eager to welcome his guests in Genesis 18:2? Do you "run" eagerly to the Lord Jesus and enjoy time with Him as He speaks to you through His written Word, the Bible, and also through prayer? What time will you choose to welcome Him each day this week?

THIRD DAY: Read Genesis 18:9-15.

1. What did the Lord tell Abraham about Sarah? Give 2 verses.

2. (Personal) God had promised Abraham offspring (seed) when he was about 75 years old (Genesis 12:2-4). He had continued making this same promise for about 24 years! See Genesis 13:14-16, Genesis 15:1-6. *Now God was fulfilling His promise.* What promise from the Bible are you trusting God for? Are you willing to wait for God's time and way to bring it to pass? If you have experienced God's faithfulness in keeping a promise from His Word, please share it with your discussion group.

3. Challenge: Why not begin to underline God's promises in your Bible today? Put your name beside them and begin to claim them for yourself. Begin with Ephesians 3:16,17; put it into your own words and share it with the class.

14

4 a. Why did Sarah laugh at what the Lord said in Genesis 18:10? What words did the Lord speak in Genesis 18:14 to encourage Sarah to trust God wholly in faith?

b. How did the angel of the Lord encourage Mary's questioning attitude (in Luke 1:26-37) when she was told that she who was a virgin would bear a child who would be the Son of God? Find the statement that is similar to what God said to Sarah in Genesis 18:14.

5 a. Did Sarah admit her lack of faith?

b. Who knew that she laughed?

6. Do you believe God graciously and lovingly helped Sarah's unbelief? See Hebrews 11:11.

FOURTH DAY: Read Genesis 18:16-33.

1. What gesture of hospitality did Abraham show in this chapter?

2. As the Lord thought about Abraham in Genesis 18:16-19, what did He say Abraham was to do for his household and his children?

3. a. Put into your own words the instructions from the Bible in the following verses to us for teaching our families about the Lord. This could be applied to teaching anyone about the Lord.

   Deuteronomy 6:6,7

   Deuteronomy 31:12

   Isaiah 28:9,10

   b. (Personal) Have you begun to put any of the instructions in these verses into practice in your family unit? If so, will you share some successful methods and the time when you do this in your family?

4 a. In this passage (Genesis 18:16-33), the Lord spoke to Abraham about Sodom, and Abraham interceded for Sodom in prayer. How many times did Abraham ask God to spare the city of Sodom? Give verses.

   b. (Personal) Does this truth encourage you to pray faithfully and expect responses from God?

5. **Challenge:** Read the following verses to help you discover what kind of a judge God is.

   1 John 4:8

Psalm 145:17

6. Do the Lord's words in Genesis 18:21 express His character as a judge?

FIFTH DAY: Read Genesis 19, concentrating on verses 1-14.

1. Lot had chosen sinful Sodom for his dwelling place (Genesis 13:8-13). What warning did the angels (Genesis 19:1) give Lot concerning the fate of Sodom? Give verse.

2. What were the reactions of Lot's sons-in-law to Lot's warning about Sodom's destruction by God?

3. In all the years Lot lived in Sodom with his family, he was unable to influence them for God. Even his daughters married ungodly men. What warning is in this incident for us in our society today?

4. Put into your own words what the following verses say concerning the Christian's relationship to the "world."
Romans 12:1,2

Galatians 1:3,4

1 John 2:15-17

5. **Challenge:** Read all of Christ's intercessory prayer in John 17 and choose some favorite verses which speak to you of His personal love for you.

6. (Personal) Will you underline in your Bible the prayer promises Christ made and claim them for your life today?

SIXTH DAY: Read Genesis 19:15-38.

1. How did God show His mercy to Lot when he "lingered," rather than obeying God's angel messengers at once?

2. Can you imagine why Lot "lingered"? Do you think he was packing his favorite possessions to take with him? Or were his wife and daughters doing this? Do you have the tendency to "linger" over worldly possessions or activities rather than to obey God when He calls you to do something?

3. **Challenge:** Read 1 Corinthians 3:10-16. Remember that Lot lost all of his possessions, land, sons-in-law, and finally his wife. Relate this to the Christian's loss as described in 1 Corinthians 3:10-16.

   a. What is the foundation the Christian is to build on?

   b. Will God ever test how we have built on this foundation?

c. Fire will burn wood, hay and stubble, but not gold, silver or precious stones (1 Corinthians 3:10-16). What kind of spiritual building material do you think Lot used while living in Sodom?

d. Once a Christian has truly received Christ as His Savior and Lord, describe what will come after his work has been tested by God.

4 a. In John 15:4,5 the Lord Jesus Christ explained how we can bring forth good works of gold, silver and precious stone. How is this possible for a Christian? Put it into your own words.

b. (Personal) Look at your life. Is your foundation your faith in Jesus Christ? If so, what kind of spiritual building materials are you using? See 1 Corinthians 3:12-15 concerning building materials. Be honest with yourself! Will they stand the test of God's holy fire?

5. How does Genesis 19 say God remembered Abraham's prayer which he prayed in Genesis 18:22-33?

6 a. What happened to Lot's wife? How did she disobey God's directions? Give verses.

b. Which verse did you choose to memorize this week?

19

GOD HONORS THOSE WHO HONOR HIM

Genesis 18—19

Study Notes

Abraham Entertains Heavenly Visitors Genesis 18:1-8

This chapter is an account of another discussion between God and Abraham. Visualize Abraham sitting at his tent door, his home, among the great oak trees of Mamre. Glancing across the desert, Abraham saw three men who were actually heavenly beings in the form of men. One of these men was the Lord, as illustrated by His own words in Genesis 18:14, "Is any thing too hard for the Lord? At the appointed time I will return to you." These words are part of a recorded conversation which took place face-to-face between the Lord and Abraham.

How calmly Abraham entertained these strangers and how calmly his entertainment was accepted! Forgetting his age of 99 years (Genesis 17:1) he ran to meet them and showed courtesy by bowing. The Bible does not tell us if he recognized them as heavenly beings, but he did see that they appeared as respectable men and therefore welcomed them hospitably into his tent home.

According to the custom of that day, he offered water to wash their feet (Genesis 18:4) and rest for them on a comfortable mat under the tree. He himself went to ask Sarah to prepare the cakes of meal and ran to the herd to fetch a tender calf which he gave to a young man to prepare for their guest's evening meal. Abraham personally set them under the tree while they ate (Genesis 18:5-8). *We can learn from Abraham an example of godly hospitality. We should take pleasure in showing kindness to anyone God sends our way.*

The Lord teaches us in many places in the Bible about Christian hospitality. We learn that a church leader loves to be hospitable (Titus 1:7,8), and all Christians are told to be hospitable to fellow Christians without grudging (1 Peter 4:9). Hebrews 13:2 also speaks to us of entertaining strangers, since it could be an angel whom God has sent to us!

Do you invite others besides close friends to your home? As the Lord leads you are you hospitable to those who are not hospitable to you? Are you willing to let your guests find you, just as you are, as Abraham's heavenly guests found him? Do you accept the fact that your house is not perfect and do the very best you can with the food you have on hand just as Abraham did?

Remember the dining room was an arbor under a tree; Abraham had no rich table linen, no sideboard set with fancy serving dishes! Whether you are a man or a woman; live in a house, apartment, or room; whether you are young or old—*the Holy Spirit will guide and teach you how to be a hospitable Christian (John 16:13,14).*

Have you ever exercised hospitality to the Lord Jesus Christ? Revelation 3:20 tells us that *Christ stands knocking at our heart's door. He wants to come in and to be our Savior and Lord, yet He will not force the door of our "home" open.* Christ has promised that He will come in and fellowship with us.

Have you ever invited the Lord Jesus Christ to be your Savior and Lord? (John 1:12; 3:16) If you are a Christian, are you as eager to have daily fellowship with the Lord as Abraham was eager to welcome his guests in Genesis 18:2? Do you "run" eagerly to the Lord Jesus and enjoy time spent with Him as He speaks to you through His written Word, the Bible, and also through prayer?

Sarah's Laughter Genesis 18:9-15

The men asked, "Where is Sarah thy wife?"

Abraham's reply was that she was in the tent. The bedouin tent of that day was divided into two parts, a closed half and an open half. The open half was the sitting room and often called "the tent door." This half was in front of the living quarters which were closed off by a dividing curtain.

Sarah was probably behind this curtain as she overheard the Lord say, "I will surely return to you about this time next year, and Sarah your wife will have a son" (18:10).

Sarah thought this news was too good to be true and she could not believe it. "So Sarah laughed to herself" (18:12). Was it a laugh of doubting and mistrust? Even where true faith is found, conflict with unbelief often exists.

Which one of us has not had such an experience of doubt and mistrust and yet still loves our Savior? An appropriate prayer for such an occasion would be, "I do believe, help my unbelief" (Mark 9:24).

The Lord knows our hearts, just as He knew Sarah's heart and realized that she had laughed within herself. (1 Samuel 16:7) God looked on her heart and saw her need to be reassured of His promise of a son. In His goodness He said, "Is anything too hard for the Lord?"

God had graciously and lovingly helped Sarah to believe His promise of a child in her old age. He will also help you with any unbelief, bitterness, depression, lust, or hate that you have in your heart. Recognize that He knows already what is there. Take it to Him in prayer, lay it all before Him, and trust Him to work in your heart as He did in Sarah's.

The angel of the Lord encouraged the virgin Mary's questioning attitude in Luke 1:26-37 when she was told that she was to be the virgin who would bear the Son of God. The angel used similar words with Mary: "For with God nothing shall be impossible."

Sarah lied about her laughter, "for she was afraid" (Genesis 18:15). The Lord saw her heart and faced her with her dishonesty by saying, "but you did laugh." This confrontation was an evidence of God's love for Sarah and was used to bring her into a position of faith to believe God's promise. In Hebrews 11:11 we read, "Through faith also Sara herself received strength to conceive seed, and was delivered of a child when she was past age, because she judged him faithful who had promised."

God had graciously and lovingly helped Sarah to believe His promise of a child in her old age. He will also help you with any unbelief, bitterness, depression, lust, or hate that you have in your heart. Recognize that He knows already what is there. Take it to Him in prayer, lay it all before Him, and trust Him to work in your heart as He did in Sarah's. "Is anything too hard for the Lord?" (Genesis 18:14).

As we consider the customs of that day, we recognize that Sarah was not done an injustice by not being included in the meal with the three guests. As was the custom then, the man of the house was the

23

host and served his guests. The wife would remain unseen in the women's quarters which was within hearing distance of the guests' table.

Abraham's wife was where she should have been. This is no declaration of inferiority. The wife and husband are one in Jesus Christ. We learn from the Bible that no man can ever be used by God in the highest way if his wife is not one with him in spiritual things (1 Timothy 3). God in His goodness reassured Sarah that He would keep His promise of a son to her, thus uniting her faith with Abraham's faith in God's promise.

Abraham's Friendship with God
Genesis 18:16-18

God talked to Abraham, His friend, and Abraham interceded for Sodom. The wickedness of Sodom had gone up before the Lord. Why did God proceed so slowly since the city was so wicked? The reason He waited was because of His longsuffering love for mankind. He waits as long as possible for men to repent of their sins, for He wants everyone to have eternal life through faith in His son (2 Peter 3:9).

The Lord stands looking at this world today just as He looked at Sodom. Christians should stand before God in the place of intercession for this world, but we must remember that He is looking at the world and the Bible tells us that a final judgment will come one day. "Will not the Judge of all the earth do right?" (Genesis 18:25).

The messengers from heaven had now finished part of their business which was an errand of grace to Abraham and Sarah. Now they had before them work of another nature. Sodom was to be destroyed. They had to announce this to Lot (Genesis 19:13). Abraham honored his guests by journeying part of the way to Sodom to show them how to reach the city. Sodom and Gomorrah were about 18 miles from Abraham's home at Hebron.

As Abraham honored the men, so we see God honoring Abraham by communicating with him as friend to friend. The Lord said, "Shall I hide from Abraham what I am about to do? Abraham will surely become a great and powerful nation, and all nations on earth will be blessed through him? For I have chosen him" (Genesis 18:17,18).

Since God had chosen Abraham to be the father of the Israelites, He wanted Abraham to have a knowledge of His character as well as His principles of justice. God's holy and righteous character would be revealed by His judgment of Sodom and Gomorrah.

The words "for I know him" or "for I have chosen him" in Genesis 18:19 reveal the intimacy of the friendship between God and Abraham. "And so it happened just as the Scriptures say, that Abraham trusted God, and the Lord declared him good in God's sight, and he was even called 'the friend of God'" (James 2:23).

In the phrase "all the nations of the earth shall be blessed in him" (Genesis 18:18) we see a definite prophecy concerning the Lord Jesus Christ. In the New Testament we read "and the Scripture, foreseeing that God would justify the Gentiles by faith, preached the gospel beforehand to Abraham, saying, 'All the nations shall be blessed in you'" (Galatians 3:8). Here is the clear announcement that the Lord Jesus Christ would come from Abraham's seed, and that He would die for the redemption of sinners who would come out of every nation.

Abraham Directs His Household
Genesis 18:19

The Lord charged Abraham with his children and his household in Genesis 18:19. He was to teach them to keep the way of the Lord by doing righteousness and justice. Family discipline is very important and is constantly spoken of throughout the Word of God as a vital part of the Christian parent's duty.

A man is not to be an elder if he does not rule his own house well (1 Timothy 3:4,5). God instructs parents to train up their children in the way they should go (Proverbs 22:6) and says that he who spares the rod really hates his son (Proverbs 13:24). Deuteronomy 6:6-9 instructs us to hide God's Word in our own hearts and teach it diligently at all times and at every opportunity. This can apply to teaching our children as well as others in our household and acquaintance.

Abraham was not to be satisfied with just giving good advice to his children, but he was to give them God's Word with real authority. There is no greater joy than to know that one's children are walking in the truth (3 John 4). *Are you instructing your children or a particular acquaintance in the ways of the Lord by teaching the Bible to them?* If you have not been fulfilling this part of God's plan for you, why not ask Him by the power of His Holy Spirit within you to guide you into doing this for your family or a friend?

A careful study of His Word will reveal all that He wants to do through you by the power of His Holy Spirit. "For it is God which worketh in you both to will and to do of his good pleasure" (Philippians 2:13). In this particular verse, the way of the Lord is righteous living in justice and in judgment. *We must all search our own hearts and ask the Lord to forgive us and completely control our hearts, minds and will so that He can reveal to us all that He wants done. He will empower us with the Holy Spirit to accomplish these things (Zechariah 4:6).*

Abraham Intercedes for Sodom
Genesis 18:20-33

We see two basic principles in God's character revealed in Genesis 18:20,21: "The outcry against Sodom and Gomorrah is so great and their sin so grievous that I will go down and see if what they have done is as bad asthe outcry that has reached me. If not, I will know."

God who is holy will not tolerate sin. He heard the cry of sin and knew about it before He judged righteously. The phrase "I will go down and see" refers to the fact that the angels disguised as men would force the Sodomites to reveal in action just how far they would go in their sin. God had already seen their sin but this was a test to show Abraham and Lot and all future generations just how many were involved in Sodom's sin. God's punishments are not based upon hearsay or gossip, but upon His own certain and infallible knowledge.

God's words challenged Abraham to intercede for Sodom. "Wilt thou also destroy the righteous with the wicked? Peradventure there be fifty righteous within the city; wilt thou also destroy and not spare the place for the fifty righteous that are therein?" (Genesis 18:23,24).

Abraham revealed his clear concept of who God really is by his statement, "Shall not the Judge of all the earth do right?" (Genesis 18:25). He showed that he understood God's willingness to forgive and grant full pardon to those who looked to him in faith. When Abraham stopped interceding, he had God's promise that He would spare Sodom if as many as 10 righteous persons could be found there. But when the required number could not be found, nothing could stop the catastrophe.

Note that Abraham's intercession was not simply for Lot's deliverance, but for all righteous men in Sodom. He clearly demonstrated genuine love and concern for his fellow man. Unselfish concern in prayer for others shines out like a jewel to God.

Do you have a prayer notebook? Have you recorded names other than those ofyour family in it? Do you have intercessory prayer times as God divinely leads you to uphold others?

Some people think indications are that God would have spared Sodom if Abraham had continued to pray. Abraham's prayer, however, seems guided by the Holy Spirit and is similar to what we can experience when wedepend upon the Spirit to guide us in prayer. "And in the same way—by our faith—the Holy Spirit helps us with our daily problems and in our praying. For we don't even know what we should pray for, nor how to pray as we should; but the Holy Spirit prays for us with such feeling that it cannot be expressed in words" (Romans 8:26).

Are you willing today to give your prayer life over to the control of the Holy Spirit? God will give you His thoughts and show you how long you should pray just as He showed Abraham.

Lot Is Warned of Sodom's Coming Destruction Genesis 19:1-14

The evil of Sodom was revealed as the two angels visited Lot. Lot was informed of the destruction to come. Here we have the account of how God "turned the cities of Sodom and Gomorrah into heaps of ashes and blotted them off the face of the earth, making them an example for all the ungodly in the future to look back upon and fear. But at the same time the Lord rescued Lot out of Sodom because he was a good man, sick of the terrible wickedness he saw everywhere around him day after day" (2 Peter 2:6,7).

These verses teach us a lesson. In all the years that Lot had lived in Sodom with his family, he was unable to influence them for God. Lot was a worldly believer who had a halfhearted love for God while loving the treasures of this world (Matthew 6:19-21; Luke 12:33,34).

Just as Lot's witness was of no avail in Sodom, so if we are halfhearted and not fully yielded to the Lord, our witness in our society will be useless.

Lot did not have close fellowship with his uncle Abraham. We need close fellowship with Christians so that we can gain strength from one another as we live in our present society. No other families in Sodom worshiped God, consequently Lot's daughters married pagan men. Children in Christian homes need to be taught the biblical principle that a Christian should not be unequally yoked to an unbeliever in marriage (2 Corinthians 6:14).

Lot chose social standing, success, wealth and comfort in a sinful city above living with those who feared and worshiped God. He could have lived near or at least honored God with Abraham. But he had chosen to live in Sodom. We, too, make a choice in our society today. What are your goals—earthly or heavenly? (Matthew 6:19-21).

Unlike Moses, Lot enjoyed the "pleasures of sin for a season" rather than to "suffer affliction with the people of God" (Hebrews 11:25). All seemed to go well for a time, but when the crisis hour came we see that Lot's whole family was tainted by the society in which they had been engulfed. Lot was warned of the approach of Sodom's ruin (Genesis 19:13) and he was directed to give notice to his friends and relatives so they could be saved with him (Genesis 19:12). Yet his sons-in-law mocked him for they thought he was making a joke (Genesis 19:14).

Even Lot's judgment had been tainted by the society around him.

27

He stooped so low as to offer his two daughters as prostitutes to the evil men who came to his door to attack the two angels. The Sodomites practiced the most abominable wickedness, a sin that still bears their name and is called sodomy. This sin is spoken of in Romans 1:26-28 and is just as abominable in God's sight today as it was in that city of Sodom long ago.

Lot's Family Departs; Sodom and Gomorrah Are Destroyed Genesis 19:15-29

Lot had opportunity to leave Sodom after he was rescued out of the enemies' hand by Abraham in Genesis 14. Yet he did not take God's warning even after he had been carried away captive by the powerful "kings of the East." He had a house in Sodom and chose to go back to the urban life of the Sodomites rather than to join Abraham in Mamre.

Today God daringly rescues men from death, illness, accident, and other disasters to prove Himself and to show Himself to us. He wants to rescue us by his mercy. Our "Lord Jesus Christ, who gave himself for our sins to rescue us from the present evil age" (Galatians 1:3,4).

The warning here is not to ignore God's deliverance and mercy to us as Lot did in Genesis 14. *God's mercy should draw us to Him in a sense of gratitude. Have you ever come to the Lord Jesus Christ in a sense of gratitude and thanked Him for what He has done for you?*

The two angels finally had to take Lot, his wife, and two daughters and lead them out of the city they had lingered in (Genesis 19:16). This showed God's mercy upon Lot, as God used the angels to remove Lot from the city. They said, "Escape for thy life; look not behind thee, neither stay thou in all the plain; escape to the mountain, lest thou be consumed" (19:17).

Lot recognized God's mercy to him and responded, "Your servant has found favor in your sight" (19:18). But Lot also realized that his strength couldn't carry him to the hills, so he asked God to provide a closer place of escape—the city of Zoar.

God agreed to allow Lot to escape there. But He urged him to hurry, "for I cannot do anything until you arrive there" (19:22). Again, God showed His mercy to Lot, assuring him that He would do Lot no harm as He destroyed Sodom and Gomorrah.

"Then the Lord rained on Sodom and Gomorrah brimstone and fire from the Lord out of heaven, and He overthrew those cities, and all the valley, and all the inhabitants of the cities, and what grew on the ground" (19:24,25). This was a definite judgment of the Lord upon people who were very sinful and who refused to be sorry for their sins.

28

God's power possibly produced an earthquake which, by opening a fissure in the rocks, released stored-up gas that exploded and hurled immense quantities of burning petroleum into the air. Undoubtedly, the action of the earthquake also caused the salt and free sulphur in the area to combine with the flaming petroleum. All that flammable material ignited, bringing about the rain of "fire and brimstone" that caused sheets of literal fire to pour upon Sodom and Gomorrah. The searing flames and black smoke, covering the whole of both cities, smothered and consumed every living thing.

The region of the two cities has always been noted for earth-quakes, and the whole Jordan Valley is part of a huge fracture in the earth's crust that continues through the Dead Sea. Jordanian officials report discovering ruins some 40 feet below the Dead Sea that are believed to be the biblical cities of Sodom and Gomorrah. They plan to drain the site and excavate those ruins.

Lot's wife made some effort to escape the impending disaster, but she let her curiosity, love of things, and love for her family cause her to disobey God's orders and look back. This was a fatal act. Her body became a pillar of salt (Genesis 19:26), probably encrusted with the deposits of the raining brimstone. The pillar stood as a warning against disobedience to a specific command of God.

Jesus sought to remind His disciples of the tragic consequences of loving mere things, and in doing so He cautioned them to "remember Lot's wife" (Luke 17:32). *His warning speaks to us today of the tragic consequences of loving the things of this world* and choosing to have them as the foundation of our lives.

"And no one can ever lay any other real foundation than that one we already have—Jesus Christ. But there are various kinds of materials that can be used to build on that foundation. Some use gold and silver and jewels; and some build with sticks, and hay, or even straw! There is going to come a time of testing at Christ's Judgment Day to see what kind of material each builder has used.

"Everyone's work will be put through the fire so that all can see whether or not it keeps its value, and what was really accomplished. Then every workman who has built on the foundation with the right materials, and whose work still stands, will get his pay. But if the house he has built burns up, he will have a great loss. He himself will be saved, but like a man escaping through a wall of flames" (1 Corinthians 3:11-15).

Verse 15 seems to describe Lot's rescue from Sodom, an eternal rescue by God. His life was all a loss, though he was saved by his faith in God, as we read in 2 Peter 2:7, "He rescued righteous Lot, greatly distressed by the licentiousness of the wicked." He escaped with his

29

life, but his life was so wasted and unimportant in God's history that even his death is not recorded for us in the Scriptures.

The Sin of Lot's Daughters; The Origin of the Moabites and the Ammonites
Genesis 19:30-38

Lot's two daughters had been soiled by the cities' shame. This last portion of chapter 19 describes incestuous relationships that we would prefer to forget. Lot's two daughters stooped low enough to engage in an act that is unspeakably sinful. They had no sense of shame over their conduct and even immortalized their sin in the names they gave their sons, for Moab means "from the father" and Ammon means "son of my people."

These descendants of Lot are later to become the enemies of Israel because of their unbrotherly conduct. Thus Lot's seed brings nothing but disaster and disgrace to him. "Be not deceived; God is not mocked: for whatsoever a man soweth, that shall he also reap" (Galatians 6:7).

What about you and me? Where do we place our values? Do we seek the things of this world and its creature comforts? Or do we seek to know God through His Son the Lord Jesus Christ and to know His plan for our lives?

Are you able to claim His strength and love for today? Can you look forward to Christ's coming again when you will stand before the judgment seat of Christ and your works will be revealed and tested by fire? (1 Corinthians 3:10-16; Romans 12:1,2).

"Abide in me, and I in you. As the branch cannot bear fruit by itself, unless it abides in the vine; neither can you unless you abide in me. I am the vine, you are the branches. *He who abides in me, and I in him, he it is who bears much fruit, for apart from me, you can do nothing*" (John 15:4,5).

Study Questions

Before you begin your study this week:
1. Pray and ask God to speak to you through His Holy Spirit each day.
2. Use only your Bible for your answers.
3. Write your answers and the verses you have used.
4. Challenge questions are for those who have the time and wish to do them.
5. Personal questions are to be shared with your study group only if you wish to share.
6. As you study look for a verse to memorize this week. Write it down, carry it with you, tack it to your bulletin board, tape it to the dashboard of your car. Make a real effort to learn the verse and its reference.

FIRST DAY: Read all of the notes and look up all of the Scriptures.

1. What was a helpful or new thought from the overview of Genesis 18 and 19?

2. What personal application did you select to apply to your own life?

SECOND DAY: Read all of Genesis 20.

1 a. Abraham left the land of Canaan just as he did in Genesis 12:10-20. What did Abraham call his wife in Genesis 12 and Genesis 20? Give verses.

b. What clue do you find in Genesis 12 which indicates why he chose to call her this? Give verses.

c. **Challenge:** Abraham was telling a half-truth about Sarah. Find the verse in Genesis 20 which speaks of this fact.

31

2 a. How did Abraham's half lie—half-truth get him into serious trouble in Genesis 20?

b. Who kept King Abimelech from making Sarah his wife and from touching her?

c. What did God promise Abimelech if he restored Sarah to Abraham, and what did He say would be the consequences if he kept her for his wife? Give verse.

d. How many people were endangered because of Abraham's half-lie?

3. Abraham's sin brought hardship and fear of death to many other people. The sin of a Christian may also bring hardship to other Christians and non-Christians. Can you think of any situations where you have seen this happen? Think of some ways in which a Christian's sin could bring a hardship to others today.

4 a. What did Abraham's sin cost Abimelech?

b. How did Abimelech rebuke Abraham for sinning against him? Give verse.

5 a. (Personal) Consider your own life carefully. Is there some secret sin or open sin which you are committing against God which is hurting yourself and others?

b. Read 1 John 1:9. What can the Christian do about his sin, and what will God do about this sin?

6 a. Challenge: We see God's goodness in protecting Abraham and Sarah in this unfortunate situation that was created by the half-lie their tongues had created. What does the Bible say concerning our tongues? Summarize the following verses in your own words.

Proverbs 10:19

James 3:3-6

b. (Personal) Do you need today to do what Romans 12:1,2 tells you to do—particularly in regard to your tongue?

THIRD DAY: Read all of Genesis 21, concentrating on verses 1-8.

1 a. What did God promise for Sarah in Genesis 17:16?

b. Did God keep His promise? See Genesis 21.

c. How old was Abraham when God set the time that Isaac would be born? See Genesis 17:1,21. About how old was Abraham when Isaac was born?

2. Did Abraham believe God's promise of a son? See Romans 4:18-21.

3. Did Sarah believe God's promise of a son? See Hebrews 11:11.

4. (Personal) Are you "fully persuaded" that God will keep His promises in the Bible to you? What promise from His Word are you currently claiming for your life?

5. **Challenge:** Read the following verses concerning God's promises in His Word and put them into your own words.

James 1:12

2 Peter 1:4

6. **Challenge:** Share some other promises from God's Word which have been helpful to you personally. Give references.

FOURTH DAY: Read Romans 4 concerning Abraham's faith in God.

1. Was Abraham justified (just as if he'd never sinned) and made righteous before God by his works or by his faith? Give verses throughout the whole chapter to prove your answer.

2. Who are the "blessed" people according to Romans 4:7,8?

3 a. Put Romans 4:21 into your own words.

   b. (Personal) Could you echo Abraham's words in Romans 4:21 and trust God in this same way for His promises to you from the Bible? Why not pray now and ask God to help you trust Him more fully this week?

4. According to Romans 4:25, why did the Lord Jesus Christ give Himself on the cross as a sacrifice and why did God raise Him from the dead on the third day?

5. If we are to receive what Romans 4:25 speaks of, what must we, like Abraham, personally have?

6. Put Romans 4:24,25 into your own words.

FIFTH DAY: Read Genesis 21:9-21.

1. In which verses does God promise Abraham that both of his sons shall live to be the fathers of nations? Which son will be the one who will produce Abraham's descendants (the Jewish race)?

2. Ishmael was the result of Sarah and Abraham's human plan to have a child. Hagar, the slave woman, would bear the son, because Sarah was barren. Ishmael represents the "fleshly efforts" of all mankind—all things done in self-will. How does Galatians 4:22,23 explain this?

3 a. **Challenge:** How does the child born to Sarah illustrate "walking in faith"?

   b. (Personal) Is there any challenge in these thoughts on the way of flesh or the way of faith for you today? Be specific and record for yourself your thoughts on this.

4. How is Galatians 5:16-24 helpful to the Christian who chooses to walk "by the spirit" of God in faith rather than walking "in the flesh" of human plans? Record in your own words the verses that you find helpful.

35

5 a. (Personal) Which fruit do you need to claim from God for your life today?

   b. How does God promise to help us in our lives (by the power of His Holy Spirit) to crucify fleshly desires and to "walk in the Spirit"? See Philippians 2:13 and share any other verses which have helped you in this area.

6 a. Because of Abraham and Sarah's disobedience in first making their own plan to provide a son through Hagar, Hagar suffered. Describe her suffering in Genesis 21 and God's goodness to her in her suffering.

   b. Describe Hagar's son, Ishmael, after reading Genesis 21:20,21.

SIXTH DAY: Read Genesis 21:22-34.

1. Shortly after Abraham sent Hagar and Ishmael away, what did Abimelech say to Abraham that would indicate that Abraham was obeying God and others noticed it?

2. (Personal) Are your neighbors, family members or business associates able to say this about you as they observe your life?

3. What did Jesus say concerning the Christian's "light" and "life"?

John 8:12

Matthew 5:16

4. What did Abraham complain to Abimelech about and what was Abimelech's reply in Genesis 21:26?

5 a. Misunderstandings often develop between friends, business associates, husband and wife, or parent and child because they do not communicate their feelings honestly to each other. What thought does Hebrews 3:13 present concerning free communication between Christians?

b. What does James 5:16 suggest about communication between Christians—and what will be the result if the advice is followed?

6 a. (Personal) Is lack of communication causing a problem in your relationship to some person? What will you do about it today?

b. Which verse did you choose to memorize and apply to your life this week?

GOD FULFILLS HIS PROMISE

Genesis 20-21

Study Notes

Abraham Leaves Canaan and Chooses to Live in Gerar Genesis 20:1-8

We saw in the two previous chapters that Abraham had close personal contact with God. We saw his unselfish courage in rescuing Lot and interceding for Sodom in Genesis 18 and 19. Yet we find recorded in Genesis 20 Abraham's self-will in leaving a place of high privilege (Canaan) for the barren wastes in Gerar (Genesis 20:1).

Why did Abraham go there? Scripture does not record this. We see here that the Bible is impartial in relating the blemishes of this most celebrated "friend of God" (James 2:23, Galatians 3:6-9).

The *predominant characteristic in Abraham's life was his faith in God*. But now the human weakness in Abraham's character is revealed as he repeats a sin of lying about his wife. He did this to protect himself just as he did in Genesis 12:10-13. Again Abraham claimed that Sarah was his sister (Genesis 20:2). Abraham was reproved of his sin in Genesis 12:17-20, but fear caused him to repeat it.

God gave us this record of the repetition of Abraham's sin to warn us. We, too, may fall into the same sin pattern when we fail to trust God with our lives and circumstances. We all have a vulnerable point where Satan can attack us and tempt us. Some areas in which we can be tempted are: criticism of others, a desire to be admired by everyone, wanting the easy way out of a situation, softheartedness when we should be firm with others, a lying or gossiping tongue, pride in always being right, depression, and worry.

These are all sins before God. But Christ has delivered us from them! The *Living New Testament* paraphrases our deliverance in this

39

way, "Since we, God's children, are human beings—made of flesh and blood—he [Jesus Christ] became flesh and blood too by being born in human form; for only as a human being could He die and in dying break the power of the devil who had the power of death. Only in that way could he deliver those who through fear of death have been living all their lives as slaves to constant dread" (Hebrews 2:14,15).

What is your weak area? Will you claim the power of the Holy Spirit as Christ dwells in you wanting to help you with your weakness today? Have you invited Jesus Christ in to be your Savior and Lord so that He can be your hope in your situation? (Ephesians 3:20).

We read that Abraham journeyed toward the territory of the Negab and dwelt between Kadesh and Shur in Gerar. The Bible gives us no clue why he left Mamre where he had lived nearly 20 years and traveled to the country of the Philistines. Gerar was in a valley on a protected inland caravan route from Palestine to Egypt (Genesis 10:19), and appears to have been a fortress city surrounded by walls built of rough boulders. It was near this spot that Abraham pitched his tent and where his servants dug wells for all of his flocks and herds.

No doubt Abimelech soon heard of Sarah's great beauty and inquired about her. "And Abraham said of Sarah his wife, She is my sister" (Genesis 20:2). It was a natural thing for the king to send for Sarah to add her to his harem, and this is exactly what he did.

Abraham was actually telling a half-truth about Sarah according to Genesis 20:12. She was his half sister. This half-lie/half-truth got him into serious trouble. The promised seed which Sarah would bare was endangered as she was taken by Abimelech to join his harem (Genesis 18:10,14).

Abraham's half-lie showed his lack of faith. "Whatsoever is not of faith is sin" (Romans 14:23). Sarah had a part in the lie, too. She said, "He is my brother" (Genesis 20:5).

Yet, God in His goodness protected Sarah's seed as He kept King Abimelech from making her his wife (Genesis 20:6). God warned him of the danger he would be in if he took Sarah to be his wife (Genesis 20:3) by telling him that the woman was already a man's wife. The penalty for this sin was death.

God in His mercy rescued us, when we were "dead in our trespasses and sins" also. *We only need to respond in faith to Him; Abimelech responded to God's warning and took a step to right the wrong which had been caused by this half-truth of Abraham's* (Ephesians 2:1-5).

Many people were endangered because of this half-lie/half-truth. Abraham was endangered, as Abimelech could have chosen to kill him for such treachery. Sarah was endangered because her seed might have become Abimelech's instead of Abraham's, which was not God's

40

plan. And Abimelech would die if he did not obey God. Also, all of Abimelech's family and servants had to die if he did not obey God.

As Abraham's sin brought hardship and fear of death to many people, the sin of a Christian may also bring hardship and fear to other Christians and non-Christians. There are many situations today where this happens—adultery, lying which defames a person's character, stealing, murder, embezzlement of funds, gossip, etc. *Such sins always cost people something.* Sheep, oxen, female and male slaves, the choice of the best land to live on and one thousand pieces of silver (verses 14-16) were given to Abraham when Abimelech restored Sarah to him.

Consider your own life carefully. Is there a lack of trust in God through some secret or open sin that is hurting not only yourself, but also others? First John 1:9 has the answer to this problem in your life.

We see here God's goodness in protecting Abraham and Sarah in this unfortunate situation created by their lie. The Bible warns us again and again, how easy it is for the tongue to create problems for those who do not, with God's help, keep it in check.

"If we put bits into the mouths of horses that they may obey us, we may guide their whole bodies. Look at the ships also; they though are so great and are driven by strong winds, they are guided by a very small rudder wherever the will of the pilot directs. So the tongue is a little member and boasts of great things. How great a forest is set ablaze by a small fire!" (James 3:3-5).

Proverbs also has much good advice on control of the tongue:

"He who keeps his mouth and tongue keeps himself out of trouble" (Proverbs 21:23).

"Death and life are in the power of the tongue" (Proverbs 18:21).

"A false witness shall not be unpunished, and he that speaketh lies shall not escape" (Proverbs 19:5).

We see that Abraham and Sarah did not escape causing much unhappiness to themselves and to others because of their lies. The same is true today.

We are also warned to keep ourselves separate from those who gossip: "He that goeth about as a talebearer revealeth secrets: therefore meddle not with him that flattereth with his lips" (Proverbs 20:19).

Each one of us needs to ask himself if he needs to do what Romans 12:1 and 2 tells him to do. *Have you yielded your tongue, the smallest muscle in your body but the most powerful, to the Lord Jesus Christ as a living sacrifice, to be controlled by the Holy Spirit's power?* Why not yield your tongue to the Lord Jesus Christ today?

Abraham and Sarah's sin of not trusting God could have been prevented if they had prayed and asked God to give them a peace in their

41

situation and a trust in His plan for their lives. *We, too, can be spared sinning because of our lack of faith if we will only bring everything to God in prayer.*

"Don't worry about anything; instead pray about everything; tell God your needs and don't forget to thank Him for his answers. If you do this you will experience God's peace which is far more wonderful than the human mind can understand. His peace will keep your thoughts and your hearts quiet and at rest as you trust in Christ Jesus" (Philippians 4:6,7).

Do you have God's peace? Do you pray about every situation in your life in faith believing that God will work it out to His honor and glory?

Abimelech Rebukes Abraham; Their Encounter Concludes with Prayer
Genesis 20:9-18

Abimelech rebuked Abraham for sinning against him (Genesis 20:9,10). He called Abraham's deception a "great sin," because it could have led Abimelech into the greater sin of adultery. Though he was a pagan king, Abimelech readily understood God's warning to him not to touch Sarah, Abraham's wife, for even in pagan cultures, people instinctively know that adultery is wrong. Such knowledge on the part of those who do not know the Word of God is another evidence that God, "in all nations . . . . had left not himself without witness" (Acts 14:16-17). Yet to their shame, many Christians treat this matter of adultery lightly in our day.

Abimelech took Abraham's action as a very great injury to himself and to his family, as they were all exposed to suffering because of another's sin. We see here that great injury is done not only to the person who sins, but to all those whose lives are touched by that sin.

In Genesis 20:11 Abraham pleaded that he tempted Abimelech to sin because he had a bad opinion of the place—"surely the fear of God is not in this place." *He tried to cover up his lack of faith by judging others. Have you ever done this?* This is a temptation which we need to take to God in prayer.

Abimelech gave a thousand pieces of silver to offset any embarrassment that Abraham and Sarah experienced when he added Sarah to his harem. Abraham was invited to choose any part of his land he wished to live in (Genesis 20:15). This was very different from the situation in Egypt in Genesis 12. The Pharaoh of Egypt ordered Abraham to leave his land after Abraham had lied to him calling Sarah his sister.

Abraham prayed for Abimelech in Genesis 20:17 and we read that the household was healed. Though Abimelech had restored Sarah, the judgment he was under had not been removed until Abraham prayed and asked God to remove it. This judgment is recorded as, "All the wombs of the house of Abimelech" were closed because of Sarah, Abraham's wife (Genesis 20:18).

The Birth and Circumcision of Isaac
Genesis 21:1-7

God kept His promise to Sarah (made in Genesis 17:15,16) that she would bear a son, be a mother of nations, and kings would come from her line. In Genesis 21:2 Sarah conceived and bore Abraham a son in his old age. We observe that God acts as He has said and as He has spoken. *His promises ring just as true to us in our lives today. We need to claim them for ourselves.*

> **Faith is committing one's whole self to the Lord Jesus Christ and trusting upon what the Word of God tells us. Abraham's body was "as good as dead," but Abraham did not look at himself. Instead he believed God's promise to him. And thus, through faith, God produced the seed He had promised, the new life within Sarah. In the same way, when we believe God's Word concerning His Son the Lord Jesus Christ and what He has done for us, God quickens us by His Holy Spirit and gives us new life within which results in new emotions and new thoughts and new decisions.**

"You won't become bored with being a Christian, nor become spiritually dull and indifferent, but you will be anxious to follow the example of those who receive all that God has promised them because of their strong faith and patience. For instance, there was God's promise to Abraham: God took an oath in his own name, since there was no one greater to swear by, that he would bless Abraham again and again, and give him a son, and make him the father of a great nation of people. Then Abraham waited patiently until finally God gave him a son, Isaac, just as He had promised" (Hebrews 6:12-15).

Isaac was born at the set time of which God had spoken to him (Genesis 18:14; 12:2). Abraham was about 100 years old when Isaac was born (Genesis 17:1,21). Through his faith in God's promise, God quickened his aged body and Sarah's aged body with new life.

Jesus spoke of a miraculous new life or a new birth in John chapter 3 which is created by the quickening power of the Holy Spirit when we come through faith to the Lord Jesus Christ. Faith is committing one's whole self to the Lord Jesus Christ and trusting upon what the Word of God tells us. Abraham's body was "as good as dead," but Abraham did not look at himself. Instead he believed God's promise to him (Romans 4:19). And thus, through faith, God produced the seed He had promised, the new life within Sarah (Romans 4:18-22).

In the same way, when we believe God's Word concerning His Son the Lord Jesus Christ and what He has done for us (John 3:16, Romans 6:23), *God quickens us by His Holy Spirit and gives us new life within which results in new emotions and new thoughts and new decisions.* Have you ever experienced this new power as you received the Lord Jesus Christ by faith? Are you sharing this good news with others?

The words that Sarah spoke about laughter in Genesis 21:6 indicate the joy that she felt as she realized that God had kept His promise to her. She had trusted Him in faith. We, too, experience this great joy and deep satisfaction as we enter into a relationship with Jesus Christ through faith, and He proves Himself to us by the presence of the Holy Spirit in our lives.

"The love of God is shed abroad in our hearts by the Holy Ghost which is given unto us" (Romans 5:5). "Now if any man have not the Spirit of Christ, he is none of his" (Romans 8:9). We know with confidence that we are Jesus Christ's when we have invited Him into our lives for, "The Spirit itself beareth witness with our spirit, that we are the children of God" (Romans 8:16).

Abraham obeyed God's instructions in Genesis 17:9,10 and 19. He named his son Isaac and circumcised him on the eighth day. The name Isaac means "laughter" and it would seem that when Abraham received the promise of him, he laughed for joy (Genesis 17:17). Now there was joy in seeing that God had fulfilled the promise. God filled Sarah with joy (Genesis 21:6) as she saw the fulfillment of His promise.

God brings mercies into our lives to encourage our joy in His work and service today, also. *For He is the author of true joy.* Jesus Christ "whom having not seen, ye love; in whom, though now ye see him not, yet believing, ye rejoice with joy unspeakable and full of glory" (1 Peter 1:8). Are you willing to share this great joy with others?

Sarah expressed her wonder in all of this by saying, "Who would have said [it]?" (Genesis 21:7). Motherhood for her was so highly improbable, so nearly impossible, that if anyone but *God had said it,* she could not have believed it.

Who would have said that God should send His Son to die for us

44

and His Holy Spirit to sanctify us, and His angel to attend us? Who would have said that such great sins could be pardoned, and such worthless creatures taken into God's great love and fellowship by His mercy through Jesus Christ our Lord?

The Expulsion of Ishmael Genesis 21:8-14

The birth of Isaac meant the beginning of conflict. Ishmael, the son born of Hagar, considered himself superior to Isaac. Sarah watched him mock and persecute her son, Isaac.

"As Isaac was, are the children of promise. But as then he that was born after the flesh persecuted him that was born after the Spirit, even so it is now" (Galatians 4:28,29). This passage in Galatians adds the detail to Genesis 21:9 where Sarah saw the son of Hagar playing with her son, Isaac.

Ishmael was the son born of mere human effort and therefore is an example of people who think they can serve God in their own way and earn their way to heaven by their own effort. Isaac represents the people who hear God's Holy Spirit speaking to them and recognize that their fallen human nature can do nothing good.

Have you ever recognized that there is no good thing within you? Have you recognized that only the Holy Spirit can do God's work through you? Can you say, "I know that nothing good dwells within me, that is in my flesh. I can will to do what is right, but I cannot do it" (Romans 7:18)?

Christians can either live a life under the law by trying to please God by outward ceremony and self-effort or they can realize that in their own selves they can do nothing. *In faith you can deliberately choose to live by the power of the Holy Spirit who will enable you to live a life which is pleasing to God.* Will you choose to trust and obey the Holy Spirit in your life and allow Him to live through you today in a way that will be pleasing to God? (Galatians 5:22,23,25).

Because of Abraham and Sarah's disobedience, sin, in first making their own plan to provide a son through Hagar, the slave, she had to suffer. In Genesis 21:10 Sarah asked Abraham to send Hagar and Ishmael away. Her request was displeasing to Abraham since Ishmael was his son in the flesh, but God asked him to do what Sarah suggested. He promised Abraham that not only would Isaac have descendants, but Ishmael would live to be the father of a nation (Genesis 21:13).

Thus Abraham was obedient to God. Early in the morning he took bread and a skin of water and gave it to Hagar and sent her away where she wandered in the wilderness of Beer-sheba. Abraham arose "early in the morning" (Genesis 21:14) to obey God's instructions.

45

Though it was contrary to his human judgment and his own inclination, he realized that this was the mind of God and made no more objections to it.

As Abraham obeyed God in casting out Hagar, we need to be obedient to God when he asks us to rid ourselves of things within our life which are displeasing to Him. "And those who belong to Christ Jesus, [the Messiah], have crucified the flesh [the godless human nature] with its passions and desires" (Galatians 5:24). Ask yourself how you can cast out the "old nature" in practical ways today!

The Deliverance of Ishmael and Hagar by God Genesis 21:15-21

As Hagar and her son wandered in the wilderness, they were reduced to great distress. A child who had been well-fed in Abraham's house now was faint from lack of food and water. No doubt, Hagar was in tears as she despaired and counted upon nothing but death for the child (Genesis 21:15,16).

God had told her before he was born that he should live to be a man, a great man, but she had forgotten this promise (Genesis 16:7-12). *Let us not forget God's promises when our circumstances grow bleak, but remember that He is faithful and will not fail us in our distress.* In this distress God graciously appeared to Hagar. The angel of God called to Hagar from heaven (Genesis 21:17) and assured her that God has seen her trouble and heard the voice of the lad under the bush where she had left him. God showed great readiness to help her.

God is always ready to help us in our trouble. *God wants to use you as an instrument to help others who are in trouble around you. Are you willing to be used by God to help someone in need this week?*

God repeated the promise concerning her son in Genesis 21:18, "I will make him a great nation." Genesis 21:20,21 shows us the type of person that Ishmael became and tells us that he lived in the wilderness of Paran. Notice that is says, "God was with the lad." God had made him, and God was with him. It is evident from this statement that God intended to fulfill His promise regarding this son of Abraham; He would make of him the great nation of the Ishmaelites. By trade he became an archer and his mother took a wife for him out of Egypt.

Abimelech Compliments Abraham Genesis 21:22-24

Abimelech paid Abraham a compliment by saying, "God is with you in all that you do" (Genesis 21:22). *His words should cause us to ask ourselves*: Do our neighbors, family members, business associates, and other people whose lives we touch look at us and say, "God is with you in all that you do"?

Christians reflect Jesus Christ to the world. "Let your light so shine before men, that they may see your good works, and glorify your Father which is in heaven" (Matthew 5:16). *If we have really chosen to let the Holy Spirit have complete control in our lives, those who touch our lives and watch us will begin to be aware that God is with us in all that we do, too!* They will accept our friendship and welcome our help when they are in need.

Are you this kind of person? Have you given yourself fully to the Lord Jesus Christ and asked the Holy Spirit to control your life?

Trouble Between Abraham and Abimelech
Genesis 21:22-34

Abraham complained to Abimelech about a well of water which Abimelech's servants had seized (Genesis 21:25). Abimelech's reply was, "You did not tell me, and I heard about it only today" (21:26). A misunderstanding had arisen because Abraham had not gone immediately to Abimelech with the problem.

Misunderstandings often develop between friends, business associates, husband and wife, or parent and child because they do not communicate freely and honestly with each other. Do you believe there could be a lack of communication with someone whom you know which is causing a problem in your relationship with that person? What can you do about this today?

The Bible tells us that we are to "exhort one another daily, while it is called To day; lest any of you be hardened through the deceitfulness of sin" (Hebrews 3:13). *James 5:16 suggests that we confess faults to one another and pray for one another—"that ye may be healed."*

If we have a lack of communication with someone the best thing to do is go to that one personally and talk about the problem. If you are unable to go in person, a phone call or a letter would be the next best step. Pray and ask the Holy Spirit to guide you and give you love before you contactthe person.

As a result of the trouble between the two men, they agreed to enter into a covenant with each other. First of all they straightened out their communication difficulties. Then Abraham gave gifts to the king to ratify the treaty. In addition to other things, he presented seven ewe lambs to Abimelech. "Thus they made a covenant at Beer-sheba" (Genesis 21:32).

Abraham planted a tamarisk tree in Beer-sheba and called on the name of the Lord, the everlasting God. God had made Himself known to Abraham in particular as his God, and remained in covenant with

47

him. Abraham went on to give glory to Him as the Lord of all. The everlasting God was before all worlds, and will be when time and days shall be no more.

"Lord, thou hast been our dwelling place in all generations. Before the mountains were brought forth, or ever thou hadst formed the earth and the world, even from everlasting to everlasting, thou art God . . . . For a thousand years in thy sight are but as yesterday when it is past, and as a watch in the night" (Psalm 90:1,2,4).

Study Questions

Before you begin your study this week:

1. Pray and ask God to speak to you through His Holy Spirit each day.
2. Use only your Bible for your answers.
3. Write your answers and the verses you have used.
4. Challenge questions are for those who have the time and wish to do them.
5. Personal questions are to be shared with your study group only if you wish to share.
6. As you study look for a verse to memorize this week. Write it down, carry it with you, tack it to your bulletin board, tape it to the dashboard of your car. Make a real effort to learn the verse and its reference.

FIRST DAY: Read all the notes and look up all the Scriptures.

1. What was a helpful or new thought from the overview of Genesis 20 and 21?

2. What personal application did you select to apply to your own life?

SECOND DAY: Read all of Genesis 22, concentrating on verses 1-3.

1. Note: In Genesis 22:1 some translations of the Bible say "God did tempt Abraham." The English words which best describe the meaning are "God did test Abraham." What does James 1:13-15 say concerning temptation by God? Put the thoughts from this passage into your own words.

2. Read the following verses to discover what the Christian can do in a time of testing in order to emerge victorious through God's strength.

Romans 6:12,13

1 Peter 5:8,9

3. How does 1 John 2:16 explain that "temptation" is not from God? What is it from?

4 a. Was Abraham listening when God spoke to him in Genesis 22:1?

   b. (Personal) Do you wake up in the morning and look to the Lord Jesus and say, "Here I am?" Do you think this expression of your awareness of His presence and your availability to Him would be a help in your life?

5 a. What did God ask Abraham to do as a test to see how obedient he would be to his heavenly Father?

   b. How did Abraham display his faith in God's guidance and plans for his life in Genesis 22:3?

6. (Personal) How obedient are you when God asks you to do something for Him? Do you move forth into the task obediently as Abraham did in Genesis 22:3? Can you think of some situations where
you have been immediately obedient and realized God's blessing
because of this? Share with your discussion group, if possible, to
encourage others.

THIRD DAY: Read Genesis 22:4-14.

1 a. How long did it take Abraham and his group to reach Moriah?

b. How many of the group did Abraham take up to the mountaintop
for worship by sacrifice?

c. What phrase in Genesis 22:5 makes you believe that Abraham
either believed that God would provide another sacrifice or that
He would raise Isaac from the dead?

d. What does Hebrews 11:17-19 say concerning this event?

2. **Challenge:** Refer to Genesis 22 and list the facts about Isaac
which show that he trusted God and did not resist being obedient
to God's orders to his father. Write the verse each item refers to.

3. Just as Abraham stretched forth his hand with the knife to slay
Isaac, what did the angel of God say to Abraham?

4. How did God provide another sacrifice for the burnt offering in
place of Isaac?

51

5. (Personal) Is there some situation in your life today which you cannot understand? Are you complaining about it or asking, "Why, God?" What could you apply to your problem from Abraham's experience to help you by faith believe God has the solution?

6. God gave Abraham this test to find out if he loved Him more than anything else in this world. In your own words, what does Romans 12:2 say concerning this?

FOURTH DAY: Read Genesis 22:15-24.

1. **Challenge:** Genesis 22:8-13 speaks of the lamb God provided for Abraham to sacrifice in place of Isaac. What do the following verses say concerning Jesus Christ? He was given as a sacrifice for sin, so that we could be forgiven and not have to suffer the consequences of our sin.

   John 1:29

   Revelation 13:8

2 a. (Personal) Have you ever invited the Lord Jesus, the Lamb of God, into your life to be your Savior? (Revelation 3:20)

   b. (Personal) Are you helping others to find Him as the Lamb of God and their Savior and Lord? What are some ways in which you could introduce people to the Lord Jesus Christ?

3. From where did the angel of the Lord call to Abraham in Genesis 22:11,15?

4. a. What blessing did the angel of the Lord promise Abraham?

b. According to Genesis 22:18, which phrase indicates what is required if we want to receive God's blessing?

c. **Challenge:** What does James 2:20-23 say concerning Abraham's obedience in faith to God's directions? Summarize this in your own words, if possible.

5. Where did Abraham go after the sacrifice to God had been completed on the mountaintop in Moriah? Find this place on a Bible map, if possible.

6. What family news did Abraham learn about his brother in Genesis 22:20-24?

FIFTH AND SIXTH DAYS: Read Genesis 23.

1 a. How long did Sarah live?

b. Where did she die? Find this on your Bible map.

2. What did Abraham request of the sons of Heth in Genesis 23?

3 a. What generous offer did the sons of Heth make Abraham? Give verse.

b. **Challenge:** What does this offer indicate to you about Abraham's reputation of character among these people?

4 a. In what place did Abraham choose to bury his wife?

b. What did he offer to pay for the place?

c. Who did this field belong to?

d. What did he offer to do in Genesis 23:11?

5 a. What did Abraham again offer to do in Genesis 23:13?

b. How much did Abraham pay for the field?

6 a. One outstanding fact about Abraham in this chapter is the respect his contemporaries in the land had for him. This should be a challenge to every Christian. How could the following verses help us to be respected as Christians by our contemporaries?

Matthew 5:16

Galatians 5:22-25

Matthew 22:37-39

b. Which verse in this lesson did you choose to memorize and apply to your life this week?

FAITH + OBEDIENCE = VICTORY AND BLESSING

Genesis 22-23

Study Notes

Abraham's Supreme Test Genesis 22:1-8

In this chapter Abraham passed God's great spiritual test of his faith. We read in Genesis 22:1, "After these things, God did tempt Abraham." This does not mean that God enticed Abraham to sin. The Hebrew word *nissa* used here means "to prove" and indicates that God was testing Abraham's faith as nothing else had yet done.

When God spoke to Abraham, his immediate reply was, "Here I am." Do you respond this same way when God calls upon you to do something? Are you available instantly? How would God grade you in obedience compared with Abraham? Remember, "to obey is better than sacrifice" (1 Samuel 15:22).

By faith Abraham obeyed (Genesis 22:8 and 9). *"You can never please God without faith, without depending on him. Anyone who wants to come to God must believe that there is a God and that he rewards those who sincerely look for him" (Hebrews 11:6).*

God recorded for us in the book of Hebrews the faith which Abraham had. "Abraham trusted God, and when God told him to leave home and go far away to another land which he promised to give him

57

Abraham obeyed. Away he went, not even knowing where he was going. And even when he reached God's promised land, he lived in tents like a mere visitor, as did Isaac and Jacob, to whom God gave the same promise. Abraham did this because he was confidently waiting for God to bring him to that strong heavenly city whose designer and builder is God . . . And so a whole nation came from Abraham, who was too old to have even one child—a nation with so many millions of people that, like the stars of the sky and the sand of the ocean shores, there is no way to count them" (Hebrews 11:8-10,12).

Truly there are great blessings that result from faith and obedience!

Perhaps after all the hardships and difficulties that Abraham had already gone through, he was beginning to think that the storm had blown over and that there would be no more trials in his life! God tested Abraham to allow him to display his faith in difficult circumstances to the praise and honor and glory of God.

We read in 1 Peter 1:7, "That the trial of your faith, being much more precious than of gold that perisheth, though it be tried with fire, might be found unto praise and honor and glory at the appearing of Jesus Christ." Just as Abraham passed through fierce fires under the greatest pressure and endured great strain to emerge in triumph, so we can count on God seeing us through any trial today!

How blessed it is to know that the Lord will supply our every need (Philippians 4:19). He will provide patience and wisdom (James 1:4-6). He will provide understanding (Psalm 119:18) and the spiritual power that you need in any test (Acts 1:8). *The Christian can emerge victorious through testing and trial by depending on God's strength, wisdom, and power!*

In Romans 6:12,13 we are told not to let sin control us, but to yield ourselves to God as instruments of righteousness. Have you yielded yourself completely to God as a tool in His hands to be used for His good purposes?

In Genesis 22:2 we hear God speaking to Abraham, "Take now thy son, thine only son Isaac." To Abraham's great amazement God was asking him to go and kill his only son by Sarah in whom the family line was to be built up. God wanted to find out by this test if Abraham loved Him more than anything else in the world.

Abraham did not question God! He did not understand why, yet he was ready to obey God instantly. He knew of God's promise that through Isaac all the nations of the earth would be blessed (Genesis 12:1-3, Genesis 17). *Abraham knew he could trust God.* He knew that should Isaac die, God would be able to raise him up!

Abraham was ready and willing to give his choicest treasure to God. Are you ready and willing to give Him your choicest treasure today?

Abraham had been brought to this point of faith by experiencing God's faithfulness in previous events. First, he was called to leave his home and relatives (Genesis 12). Second, God asked him to separate himself from Lot because of the strife over the grazing land for cattle. Abraham obeyed God in each of these ways.

God called him to a further step of commitment in Genesis 14. He went into battle to deliver Lot from imprisonment by kings who had swept down into the land where he lived and conquered the people who lived there, including Lot and his family. Abraham not only delivered Lot but also the people of the area and refused to accept any spoil from the battle. He did not want any of the local kings to say, "I have made Abram rich" (Genesis 14:23). For he knew that he could trust God to keep him!

Abraham then moved on in another step of faith as he prayed for Sodom and saw God deliver Lot and his daughters from the fires that rained down from heaven because of the sin in the place (Genesis 18-19). In Genesis 21 we have recorded another step of faith for Abraham as he obeyed God by sending away his son, Ishmael, by the slave girl, Hagar.

Thus we see that Abraham moved from one step of faith to another throughout his lifetime. Perhaps you are worried that God may ask you to do something that you are unable to do in faith. *Remember that whatever God asks you to do He will give you the power to do it!* God has promised that He will never allow us to be tempted above and beyond what we are able to bear (1 Corinthians 10:13). We can depend upon this promise!

We need not be afraid, for we can count on the fact that "God hath not given us the spirit of fear; but of power, and of love, and of a sound mind" (2 Timothy 1:7). If you are a Christian, you have the Holy Spirit living within you to give you power (Acts 1:8). You can count upon the promise that "it is God which worketh in you both to will and to do of his good pleasure" (Philippians 2:13).

Just as Abraham could follow God's leading by faith step-by-step, so you, too, by faith can follow God's leading in your life without fear. Psalm 37:23,31 tells us "The steps of a good man are ordered by the Lord: and he delighteth in his way . . . The law of his God is in his heart; none of his steps shall slide."

God is asking you to step out in faith today in some way. Perhaps that step of faith needs to be taken in your heart by asking the Lord Jesus Christ to be your Lord and Savior. Perhaps that step of faith has something to do with your job, your home, your relationships with others, your attitudes within your family, a situation in your neighborhood or office, or a need in your church. Are you willing to trust God all the way step-by-step, just as Abraham did?

Abraham is told to offer his only son. This is a small picture of the heavenly Father offering His only Son, Jesus Christ, as a sacrifice on the cross for our sin (John 3:16-17).

Abraham was told to go the land of Moriah (Genesis 22:2) to make the burnt offering sacrifice. Moriah means "chosen by God." This Moriah, one of the hills in what eventually became Jerusalem, is probably the same site where Solomon built the Temple and where sacrifices were then offered.

"Then Solomon began to build the house of the Lord in Jerusalem on Mount Moriah, where the Lord had appeared to his father David, at the place that David had prepared, on the threshing floor of Ornan the Jebusite" (2 Chronicles 3:1).

In a later Temple on this same Moriah, at the moment His Son Jesus Christ died on the cross, God ripped the Temple veil in two (Matthew 27:51; Mark 15:37-39). That veil hung before the Holy of Holies where previously only the High Priest met with God. God's tearing the veil during the Crucifixion meant that His Son's death had opened the way to God for all men and that anyone who would receive Jesus Christ by faith would always have direct access to God through His Son (Hebrews 10:19-22).

However, in Abraham's day this place was uninhabited. Abraham could not have foreseen Jerusalem with its temple or Calvary, but God saw them!

We read in Genesis 22:3 that Abraham rose up early in the morning to obey God. He saddled his ass and took two servants with him as well as his own son. He even cut some wood for the burnt offering and left for Moriah.

Such obedience in faith is described in Psalm 119:60, "I hasten and do not delay to keep thy commandments." Abraham did not delay, deliberate or debate. This is an example to us that when God makes His will known to us we should do it speedily without delay. When we wait, time is lost and sometimes our heart grows hard.

Abraham didn't sit down and complain about the situation and ask, "Why, God?" He didn't ask, "How can I ever look Sarah in the face again?" He didn't wonder what the Egyptians and the Canaanites and the Perizzites who dwelt in the land would say! These and many similar objections could have been made, yet Abraham recognized that here was a command of God and this was sufficient enough reason for him to step out in faith.

Is there some situation in your life today which you cannot understand? Has God called you to step out in faith in some way concerning it? God is calling you to believe in faith that He will take you step-by-step through whatever He is calling you to do according to His will.

How obedient are you when God asks you to do something for

Him? Are you aware of the Lord Jesus Christ's presence with you early in the morning? He wants to use you and lead you from faith to faith daily, moment by moment, just as He did Abraham. Have you said, "Yes, God, here I am; use me," yet today? Why not stop and do this right now?

Abraham and Isaac and the servants traveled for three long days. At last Mt. Moriah, of which God had spoken, came into sight. Abraham said to his servants, "Stay here with the donkeys; the lad and I will go yonderand worship, and we will come back to you" (Genesis 22:5). The servants were probably not permitted to accompany them, for they might have opposed the sacrifice of Isaac.

Faith must always go alone with God. God wants us to abandon our hearts to Him and to leave behind the doubts which would limit His acting for us in a particular situation. What doubt do you need to leave behind as you climb up your mountain in faith? (Mark 11:23).

Thus Abraham and Isaac went on up the mountain together. By this time Isaac was a young lad. We do not know how old he was, but the Hebrew word which is translated "lad" is also used for armed soldiers.

Opinion differs here on whether Isaac knew before arriving at Moriah that he was to be the sacrifice. Those who feel he did know would also have us note then how willing he was to be sacrificed. Such an attitude on Isaac's part reflects the attitude of Christ who said, "For this reason the Father loves me, because I lay down my life, that I may take it again. No one takes it from me, but I lay it down of my own accord. I have power to lay it down, and I have power to take it again; this charge I have received from my Father" (John 10:17,18).

Thus Isaac's obedience to his father illustrates Jesus Christ's perfect obedience to God the Father. Abraham was 100 years older than Isaac. If Isaac had refused to bear the wood, Abraham could not have forced him. However, Isaac willingly carried the wood just as Christ willingly carried His wooden cross.

Isaac said, "The fire and the wood are here, but where is the lamb for the burnt offering?" (Genesis 22:7).

Abraham replied, "My son, God will provide himself a lamb" (Genesis 22:8). The Hebrew verb here means "to see." Abraham was saying that God in His own way would see that a lamb was provided.

Some Bible scholars believe Abraham had an inner conviction that in some way God would do something about the matter when they reached the top of the mountain. Other scholars are of the opinion that Abraham expected to slay his son, but that God would in some way bring Isaac back from the dead. They base part of their conviction for this upon Abraham's words in Genesis 22:5, "I and the lad will go yonder and worship, and come again to you." Since Isaac appears to be a type of Christ because he is an only son and is to be offered up by the sacrifice, it is fitting that Abraham would believe that God was able to raise Isaac from the dead (Hebrews 11:17-19).

In Genesis 22:7 and 8, both Isaac and Abraham speak of a lamb for the burnt offering about to be sacrificed, probably because the lamb was commonly used as a sacrificial animal by God's people. Jesus Christ is the Lamb which God provided as a sacrifice for our sins on the cross in place of punishing us for our sins. He was given as a sacrifice for sin so that we could be forgiven and not have to suffer the consequences of our sin.

John 1:29, "Behold the Lamb of God, which taketh away the sin of the world." Jesus Christ was "the lamb slain from the foundation of the world" (Revelation 13:8). God planned from the beginning of the world and before that time to give Jesus Christ, His only Son, upon the cross. In Isaiah 53:6,7 we read that we have all gone astray and the Lord laid on Christ all of our sin. These verses tell us that He was brought as a lamb to the slaughter.

God sent His only Son into the world so that we might live through him (John 3:16,17; 1 John 4:9,10). This is the great love by which God loved us even before the world began. Have you thanked God today for this great love which He has for you?

God Provides a Ram Genesis 22:9-14

When they reached the place of sacrifice, Abraham must have told Isaac why they had come. Then he built an altar, laid the wood in order, bound Isaac and placed him upon the wood. Again we see Isaac's willingness to be a sacrifice, portraying as a visual aid for us Christ's willingness to die upon the cross for sin.

"Be full of love for others, following the example of Christ who loved you and gave himself to God as a sacrifice to take away your sins. And God was pleased, for Christ's love for you was like sweet perfume to him" (Ephesians 5:2).

Christ was the final fulfillment of all the sacrifices which had been offered up to God for sin. After His death on the cross, there was no further need for such sacrifices. As an act of thanksgiving for Christ's willingness, we are instructed by God in Romans 12:1 to present our "bodies a living sacrifice, holy, acceptable unto God." *Have you given yourself back to God as a living sacrifice by placing your faith in His Son, the Lord Jesus Christ? Are you sharing these great truths with others today?*

Just then the angel of the Lord called to Abraham by name from heaven. Abraham was listening, and the instant he heard his name, he said "Here am I!" (Genesis 22:11).

The angel of the Lord in the Old Testament often represents the second person of the Trinity, the Lord Jesus Christ. The angel said "Lay not thine hand upon the lad, neither do thou any thing unto him: for now I know that thou fearest God" (22:12).

The best evidence of our love for God is our willingness to serve and honor Him with all which is dearest to us, be it reputation, possessions, friendship or family. Are you willing to put God ahead of any of these things in your life?

By faith, Abraham was called the "friend of God" (James 2:23). What is faith? Faith is believing what you cannot see. It is believing so much that you will act upon your belief. If we have faith such as Abraham had, nothing is too hard for us to bear nor too great for us to do. And most important of all, we are "friends of God."

Then Abraham looked up and saw behind him a ram caught in a thorny bush by his horns. God provided the burnt offering! (Genesis 22:13). Abraham committed his son to the hand of his loving Lord. He trusted God and God provided the ram in place of Isaac.

Never be afraid to put your life into God's hand. He will always take care of you. "But my God shall supply all your need according to his riches in glory by Christ Jesus" (Philippians 4:19). And so Abraham called that place "Jehovah-jireh" which means "the Lord will provide."

God Repeats His Blessing to Abraham Genesis 22:15-24

Abraham's faith was so deep, so strong, that he instantly obeyed God. By faith Abraham was called the "friend of God" (James 2:23). What is faith? *Faith is believing what you cannot see. It is believing so much that you will act upon your belief. If we have faith such as Abraham had, nothing is too hard for us to bear nor too great for us to do. And most important of all, we are "friends of God."*

The angel of the Lord called to Abraham the second time from heaven and told him that because he had been obedient in faith, God would bless him. "I will indeed bless you, and I will multiply your

63

descendants as the stars of heaven and as the sand which is on the seashore. And your descendants shall possess the gates of their enemies, and by your descendants shall all the nations of the earth bless themselves, because you have obeyed my voice" (Genesis 22:17,18). Thus God renewed and ratified His covenant with him which had been related to him in Genesis 12:1-3; 13:16; 15:5,6; 15:17-21; 17:1-8; and 18:17-19.

The ultimate fulfillment of "in thy seed shall all the nations of the earth be blessed" (Genesis 22:18) would take place when Christ died willingly to redeem all people of faith. Thus through Christ the promise of forgiveness becomes available even to the Gentiles who were not a chosen people. The final fulfillment of this text will come when Christ comes again and "the earth shall be full of the knowledge of the Lord, as the waters cover the sea" (Isaiah 11:9).

All these blessings promised to Abraham, blessings regarding the number of descendants, victory over physical enemies, and spiritual blessings to all people were a result of his obedient faith—"because you have obeyed my voice" (Genesis 22:18). *Are you daily listening to the voice of God as you read the Bible, His Written Word, and as you communicate with Him in prayer?*

The importance of obedience cannot be overestimated. When we obey God without question we have His blessing and His wisdom. As we demonstrate this obedience, we discover that His plans are best for us and that He is full of loving kindness and is wonderfully good to us.

Have you begun to trust God for the same blessings that He gave to Abraham because of his faith and obedience? Why not stop now and commit yourself in faith and obedience to the Lord Jesus Christ?

Abraham, the friend of God, returned to Beer-sheba where he lived (Genesis 22:19). It had taken approximately three days to walk to the land of Moriah, and it probably took the same length of time to return to Beer-sheba. He and Isaac must have been aglow with the sense of God's presence and goodness. They would never be the same again.

God had assured them that the covenant blessings would come upon Abraham and his descendants. They were looking forward to what was to come from God. Abraham was going down the hill to sorrow and death (Sarah's death), but his vision was filled with heavenly things and God would give him a quiet time as he said good-bye to Sarah, his beloved wife of many years.

In Genesis 22:20-24 a paragraph about Abraham's distant family is inserted which tells us about Nahor, Abraham's brother and his offspring. In Genesis 22:23 we note that Rebekah is the granddaughter of Nahor. Thus we see that Rebekah, who is to become Isaac's wife, is the grandniece of Abraham.

The Death and Burial of Sarah
Genesis 23:1-20

The place where Sarah died was Kirjath-arba, which is Hebron in the land of Canaan (Genesis 23:2) and it is also known as Mamre and Machpelah. Abraham was either away from home when Sarah died or the phrase "and Abraham came to mourn for Sarah" means that he came into the tent where her body lay. Sarah had been a real woman of faith (Hebrews 11:11,12) and Abraham had deep sorrow at their parting.

Sarah was 90 when her son Isaac was born. She died nearly 40 years later at the age of 127 (Genesis 23:1). She had been a good mother to Isaac and he missed her very much. We see that Isaac was comforted later in Genesis 24:67 when he married Rebekah.

The Hittites were scattered throughout Canaan for many centuries of Israel's history. Abraham was considered a stranger in their country. The sons of Heth made a generous offer to give Abraham any of their family graves in which to bury Sarah (Genesis 23:6). Abraham expressed his faith in God's promise to give him this land by insisting on purchasing a piece of ground for a grave for Sarah and for all others of his family in this land of Canaan.

Instead of taking Sarah's body back to Ur of the Chaldees, Genesis 11:31, or to Haran, Genesis 11:32, Abraham chose to buy a piece of land for her grave in Canaan, the land that God had given him. Thus he expressed his faith in God's promise. He selected land in the field of Ephron in Machpelah (Genesis 23:17) which had the cave in which Sarah was buried. This cave became a burial site not only for Sarah, but for Abraham, Isaac, Rebekah, Jacob, and Leah. In later years it became a Muslim possession and today a mosque is claimed to have been built upon this site.

Thus we see that Abraham revealed his faith in God's promises by remaining in Canaan after Sarah's death. Abraham was an honorable man. The Hittites called him "a mighty prince among us" (Genesis 23:6). *So we see that his contemporaries who did not share his faith respected him highly. Do your contemporaries in business, in your church, in your home, in your neighborhood and in your community respect you because of your faith and obedience to the Lord Jesus Christ?*

As a Christian you have the opportunity to reveal the love of Jesus Christ to the world! Do you love the Lord first and love your neighbor as yourself? (Matthew 22:37-39). Only as you trust in the Lord Jesus Christ and obey His leading can He help you to accomplish this.

Study Questions

Before you begin your study this week:
1. Pray and ask God to speak to you through His Holy Spirit each day.
2. Use only your Bible for your answers.
3. Write your answers and the verses you have used.
4. Challenge questions are for those who have the time and wish to do them.
5. Personal questions are to be shared with your study group only if you wish to share.
6. As you study look for a verse to memorize this week. Write it down, carry it with you, tack it to your bulletin board, tape it to the dashboard of your car. Make a real effort to learn the verse and its reference.

FIRST DAY: Read all of the notes and look up all of the Scriptures.

1. What was a helpful or new thought from the overview of Genesis 22 and 23?

2. What personal application did you select to apply to your own life?

SECOND DAY: Read all of Genesis 24, concentrating on verses 1-9.

1. List all of the things you learn about Abraham and his servant in Genesis 24:1,2.

2. Abraham, according to the ancient custom of confirming an oath, had his servant put his hand under his thigh. What was the oath (promise) which Abraham had the servant make?

3. **Challenge:** Abraham did not want his son to marry someone who did not worship the Lord. The Bible has many instructions con-

cerning marriage. *Summarize* in your own words what the following verses teach concerning marriage.

Ezra 9:11,12

Proverbs 18:22

Mark 10:6-9

4. Who was to guide Abraham's servant on the journey and where was he to go to look for a wife for Isaac? Give verses in Genesis 24.

5. Read Hebrews 1:7-14. Do you think God ministers to us through angels today?

6. If the woman to whom the angel led Abraham's servant would not return, what was the servant to do?

THIRD DAY: Read Genesis 24:10-14.

1. **Challenge:** According to the custom of that day, Abraham was acting as a godly man by seeing to it that the proper wife was chosen for his son, Isaac. Put into your own words what the following verses say about parents' responsibilities to their children.

Deuteronomy 6:4-7

Proverbs 29:15,17

67

2. What did the servant take with him on his journey to find a wife for Isaac, and where did he go?

3. When he arrived at his destination, did he depend upon his own wisdom to find Isaac's wife? Give the reason for your answer.

4. (Personal) Do you pray and ask God for guidance in your life or do you make your plans first and then ask God to bless them? Which do you think is God's plan for you?

5. What does Proverbs 3:5,6 say concerning God's guidance and help to the Christian?

6. What sign did the servant ask God to give him to reveal which maiden should be Isaac's wife? See Genesis 24.

FOURTH DAY: Read Genesis 24:15-32.

1. What was the name of the girl who came out with her water jug, and what relationship did she have to Abraham? See Genesis 22:20-23 also.

2. Try to describe Rebekah from this passage. Give verses.

3. What did the servant give Rebekah and what did he ask her?

4. Did the servant remember to thank God for answering his prayer concerning a wife for Isaac? Give verses.

5. We are to give thanks to God. What do the following verses say about giving thanks? Do you thank God in these ways?

   Hebrews 13:15

   1 Thessalonians 5:18,19

   Colossians 4:2

6. What was Rebekah's brother's reaction to this stranger at the well?

FIFTH DAY: Read Genesis 24:33-49.

1. What did Abraham's servant do before he would eat the food set before him?

2. What do you learn about God's help, and man's worship and thanksgiving from Genesis 24:48?

3. (Personal) How do you apply question 2 to your particular problems or responsibilities this week?

4. **Challenge:** We see from Genesis 24:33-49 that the business of the Lord demands priority over hunger or any other circumstances in our lives. What do the following verses say which encourage us to put God first? Put them into your own words if possible.

John 4:32, 34

Isaiah 40:31

2 Chronicles 20:15, 17

5. What decision did the servant ask Rebekah's brother, Laban, and father, Bethuel, to make? Give verse.

6. (Personal) Which was your favorite verse in question 4 of today's study? Share with your group and give the reason why, if possible.

SIXTH DAY: Read Genesis 24:50-67.

1. What was Laban and Bethuel's response to the servant's request for Rebekah as a bride for Isaac?

2. Abraham wanted a godly wife for his son. He planned for this. In what ways can a parent encourage his child to marry a Christian? How young do you think parents should start talking to their child about this, since in our culture the child selects his mate rather than the parent?

3 a. How soon did the servant want to take Rebekah back to Abraham?

b. How long did her brother and mother want her to remain with them before she made the trip?

c. What was Rebekah's decision about the trip?

d. Who went on the journey with Rebekah other than Abraham's servants?

4. **Challenge:** Rebekah's decision to come immediately to her husband-to-be can be compared to a person who comes to the Lord Jesus Christ in faith at once after hearing the good news of Jesus Christ. Who could Abraham's servant be compared to? Who could Rebekah's nurse and maids be compared to?

5. Because God had chosen Isaac and Rebekah to be man and wife, what does Genesis 24:62-67 tell you that they had in their marriage?

6 a. (Personal) God has chosen you to be His child by faith. If you come to Him as Rebekah made haste to go to Isaac, God has many blessings in store for you, including His wonderful love. Have you come? (John 1:12 and Revelation 3:20)

71

b. (Personal) If you are a Christian, are you being God's faithful servant, just as Abraham's servant was faithful? What are some different ways that you can bring others back to God?

c. What verse did you choose to memorize and put into practice in your life this week?

THE FATHER'S CARE REFLECTS THE FATHER'S LOVE

Genesis 24

Study Notes

Abraham Directs His Faithful Servant Genesis 24:1-9

Abraham was probably about 140 years old (Genesis 21:5; 25:20) when he set out to arrange a wife for Isaac. Isaac was about 40 years old, which was well beyond the customary age of his ancestors for marriage (Genesis 11:14-24). Abraham wanted to make sure before he died that Isaac chose a wife from his own people (Genesis 24:3,4), rather than from the pagan Canaanites among whom they were dwelling. The Lord had blessed Abraham in all things (Genesis 24:1) and he was now trusting Him to bless his son with a good wife.

Abraham chose his eldest servant to make the long journey to Mesopotamia to the city of Nahor (Genesis 24:10). The main objective of the trip was that Isaac's bride be from Abraham's own family. Abraham asked his servant to take a vow, an ancient custom for confirming a solemn oath (Genesis 24:9). By putting a hand under a man's thigh, a person promised that if he did not keep the oath, the unborn children would have the right to avenge this act of unfaithfulness.

The servant who took this oath was probably Eliezer whom we met in Genesis 15:2. At that time Abraham wanted to make him his heir, as was the custom of the day in a household where no children had been born. Because he was elderly we know that he had lived long enough with Abraham to see that God answered his prayers and helped him through all of the years. He had undoubtedly witnessed the miraculous birth of Isaac when Abraham was 100 years old. Therefore, this servant likewise believed that God would help him keep his oath to his godly master, Abraham.

Abraham assured the servant of God's help: "He shall send his angel before thee, and thou shalt take a wife unto my son from thence" (Genesis 24:7). *The confidence that Abraham put in God gave the servant confidence in the success of this undertaking.*

As we come to the Lord Jesus Christ in faith, we, too, can have confidence that God will show us the way and send His angel before us to guide and direct our lives. When we sincerely aim to bring glory to the name of God through our lives, we have the comfort of knowing that His angels will minister in our lives. Hebrews 1:14 speaks of angels as "ministering spirits, sent forth to minister for them who shall be heirs of salvation."

The Lord Jesus Christ also promised the comfort of the Holy Spirit, "for He dwelleth with you" (John 14:17), and "He shall teach you all things, and bring all things to your remembrance" (John 14:26). We have the promise of the constant presence of the Holy Spirit which Abraham and his servant did not have (before Jesus Christ came to earth and then returned to heaven). Thus we have more of God's help and encouragement than the servant of Abraham had!

Are you relying on God's help in every area of your life—your personal relationships, your home, your business, and in all the affairs of this life? Why not stop to pray now and commit to God the area of your life where you have a need. He is waiting to go before you just as He went before Abraham's servant on the journey to Mesopotamia.

According to the custom of that day, Abraham was acting as a godly man by seeing that a proper wife was chosen for his son, Isaac. *The Bible teaches us that godly parents have many responsibilities to their children.* Though we do not choose our child's mate in our particular culture, we have other responsibilities for which we will be held accountable to God.

There are wise instructions for us in Deuteronomy 6:4-7. These words were spoken to Israel, but also can be applied to those of us who worship the Lord Jesus Christ today. "Jehovah is our God, Jehovah alone. You must love him with all your heart, soul, and might. And you must think constantly about these commandments I am giving you today. You must teach them to your children and talk about them when you are at home or out for a walk; at bedtime and the first thing in the morning."

Yes, we are to teach our children of the Lord! Much emphasis is put on secular education today; parents would not think of neglecting to send their children to school. How much more important is their Christian education!

A Christian parent should not depend upon the Sunday School to provide the total Christian education for his child. Children need to be surrounded by an atmosphere of trust and joy in the Lord. They need to see their parents delight in God's Word. A parent's attitude is caught!

"How sweet are thy words unto my taste! yea, sweeter than honey to my mouth! Through thy precepts I get understanding: therefore I hate every false way" (Psalm 119:103,104).

The Bible also gives many instructions for disciplining our children in love. God disciplines the child of faith that He loves. "The Lord reproves him whom he loves, as a father the son in whom he delights" (Proverbs 3:12).

Proverbs 29:15 and 17 add further light to a Christian parent's role in discipline. "The rod and reproof give wisdom: but a child left to himself bringeth his mother to shame . . . Correct thy son and he shall give thee rest; yea, he shall give delight unto thy soul."

The love of Christ should be shown in all of our discipline as Ephesians 6:4 says, "Fathers, provoke not your children to wrath; but bring them up in the nurture and admonition of the Lord." *Christian parents are responsible to be firm, yet tender and loving in their discipline. It is essential that they pray for guidance before making decisions concerning discipline of their children.* Do you pray to your heavenly Father and ask for guidance in raising your children?

As a Christian you may have "spiritual children" who come to faith in Jesus Christ through your sharing of the Good News. These same principles apply in your attitude toward a "spiritual child." Whether the child be "of the flesh" or "spiritual," you will want him to be able to choose God's way for his life. This may involve the choice of a life partner, but also will involve other things.

The groundwork for such choices must begin very early in the life of a new Christian. You as a "spiritual parent" are responsible to train the new Christian with the principles of the Christian life found in the Bible. In fact, you can't begin too early!

The moment a child is able to hear and observe his parents, his training concerning the Lord Jesus Christ has begun. In our present culture one could almost throw up his hands in despair and say, "How can I compete with this wicked society and all of the temptations that my children face as a result of it?"

Remember that the God who worked for Abraham and blessed him as he lived in the midst of the pagan society of the Canaanites also

75

loves you. He is waiting to bless and guide you in the training of your children. "Except the Lord build the house, they labour in vain that build it" (Psalms 127:1). Trust God to guide you.

The servant asked Abraham what he should do if the maiden was not willing to return with him into Abraham's land. He asked if he should take Isaac out of Canaan to Nahor (Genesis 24:5). Abraham very clearly stated that Isaac was not to be taken out of Canaan to select a wife.

Perhaps he feared that Isaac would enjoy being with his relatives so much that he would not return to Canaan, the land which God had promised to Abraham and his seed. By keeping Isaac there he was probably making sure that his descendants would possess the land of Canaan. "To your descendants I will give this land" (Genesis 24:7). If the woman was not willing to return with the servant, he was to be freed from his oath by Abraham (Genesis 24:8). Thus with all the instructions given to the servant, the oath was formally sworn to and the servant was ready to go.

The Servant Prays for Guidance
Genesis 24:10-14

Abraham ordered his servants to load 10 of his finest camels with provisions and gifts for the bride and her family. In a way these gifts would make up for the loss of such a beloved member of the family as Rebekah. It was the custom to present valuable gifts to members of the bride's family. This custom continued on to the time of Hammurabi (1728-1686 B.C.) when the bride was actually purchased by the groom's family.

As Abraham's servant prepared for the journey of over 400 miles across the desert, his men carefully wrapped and tied on the camels' backs presents of gold earrings and bracelets, silver jewelry, and beautiful clothes. They also packed great packages of food and filled many goat skin bottles with water for their journey. It must have been quite a sight to see this caravan of 10 camels, each piled high with bundles, bags, and goat skin bottles, with their drivers plodding along by their sides! Those who would meet this caravan along the way would certainly be impressed with Abraham's wealth and importance. This large company would also be a defense against robbers and bandits, who made travel dangerous in that country.

After days of traveling across the hot sand, the servant and his caravan arrived at just about sunset at the city of Nahor (which may have been the same as the city of Haran). "And he made his camels to kneel down without the city by a well of water at the time . . . that women go out to draw water" (Genesis 24:11).

76

Before anyone came, the servant did the right thing. He asked the Lord to give him a sign by which he would know the girl he must select for Isaac's wife. *He did not depend upon his own wisdom to find Isaac's wife, but went to God in prayer and asked Him to lead him to the right maiden.* The servant could have asked the first man he met where Abraham's relations lived, and gone directly to their house! Yet he knew that the choice was to be God's, and that the angel of the Lord was leading him. He was willing to wait upon God and not attempt to use human means to bring about God's plan.

It is so important for us today to take the example of the servant and use it in our lives! We are prone to make our own little plans first and then ask God to bless them. Yet, God cannot bring about His plan in our lives this way. Do you pray and ask God for guidance in your life, or do you make your plans first and then ask God to bless them?

We can learn much from the servant's attitude and his prayer. First of all he prayed, "O Lord God of my master Abraham." He knew that Abraham loved God and that God loved Abraham.

We are instructed to pray "in Jesus' name" because we love Him and He loves us. "If ye shall ask anything in my name, I will do it" (John 14:14; 15:16). As a Christian do you end your prayer by saying, "In Jesus' name?" By praying in Jesus' name, you make a deliberate choice of faith and show your confidence in the Lord Jesus Christ.

The servant asked God to bless him and his master Abraham "this day." This reminds us of the prayer that Jesus taught His disciples. "Thy will be done in earth, as it is in heaven. Give us this day, our daily bread" (Matthew 6:10,11).

The servant's prayer was as practical as asking for daily bread! He asked that God would identify the woman by her willingness to give both him and his camels a drink of water. His prayer was a prayer of faith, for he said, "By this I shall know that thou hast shown steadfast love to my master" (Genesis 24:14).

He truly believed that God was going to answer his prayer. When you pray, do you have this same confidence that God will answer your prayers? "All things, whatsoever ye shall ask in prayer, believing, ye shall receive" (Matthew 21:22).

The Servant Meets Rebekah at the Well
Genesis 24:15-33

Before his prayer was even finished, a beautiful girl named Rebekah came to the well to draw water. She was carrying a pitcher upon her shoulder. The Bible says, "The maiden was very fair to look upon, a virgin, whom no man had known" (Genesis 24:16). She was beautiful and no doubt looked as sweet and kind as she was beautiful.

The servant must have hoped she would be the chosen one. He ran to meet her after she had filled her pitcher and said, "Let me, I pray thee, drink a little water of thy pitcher" (24:17).

Rebekah quickly took down the pitcher and gave him a drink. Then she volunteered to draw water for the 10 camels until they had quenched their thirst—no easy task for Rebekah to do. Those camels had come a long way across the desert and were very thirsty. The Bible says that she ran again to draw water for the camels.

You may wonder if God can guide you in the same way He guided Abraham's servant long ago. He works in the very same way today. Just as God brought Rebekah to the servant as a proof of His guidance, God also uses circumstances to show us how He is answering our prayers.

The servant stood wondering at her (24:21), probably amazed that she was willing to do so much, for she must have drawn about 200 gallons to satisfy all the camels. Many times she let her jar down into the well and then poured water into the trough for the camels to drink. Rebekah's kind act revealed an attitude of helpfulness and thoughtfulness. It also demonstrated that she was energetic, a fast worker—and certainly not lazy.

When the camels had finished drinking, the servant gave the maid the golden jewelry he had brought (24:22). He asked, "Whose daughter art thou? . . . Is there room in thy father's house for us to lodge in?" (24:23).

Rebekah told him there was room for them and that she was the granddaughter of Nahor, Abraham's brother—making her Abraham's grandniece!

The servant knew for certain then that she was the one to be Isaac's bride. At once he bowed his head and worshiped the Lord (24:26,27). He never forgot to pray.

We need to recognize God's clear guidance in answer to our prayers and to thank Him for this! It is so human to ask for something and then take all the credit for His answer to the prayer or to think that it is just "coincidence" that things turned out so well. Hebrews 13:15 teaches us to continually praise God by giving thanks to His name. First Thessalonians 5:18,19 suggests that we thank God in all things so that the Spirit is not quenched!

Not only are we to give thanks to God, but according to Psalm 105:1,5 we are to, "Give thanks unto the Lord; call upon his name: make known his deeds among the people . . . . Remember his mar-

78

velous works that he hath done; his wonders, and the judgments of his mouth." *We should share answers to prayer with others, so they may see how God is at work in our world today. Are you doing this?*

You may wonder if God can guide you in the same way He guided Abraham's servant long ago. He works in the very same way today. Just as God brought Rebekah to the servant as a proof of His guidance, God also uses circumstances to show us how He is answering our prayers.

Today we have the Word of God to test circumstances, making sure that they coincide with God's principles. The Holy Spirit makes us aware, by the peace He gives us, of God's answer to prayer and of His plan for our lives. God can guide us through His ordering of our circumstances, His Word and the peace of the Holy Spirit.

Rebekah hurried home and told her mother and family about the stranger. Her brother, Laban, went out to the well and said, "Come in, thou blessed of the Lord; wherefore standest thou without? for I have prepared the house, and room for the camels" (Genesis 24:31). As was the custom of that day, Laban provided water to wash the feet of the servant and the men with him, and set food on the table for them.

However, the servant felt that God's business had to come before his pleasure and said, "I will not eat, until I have told mine errand" (Genesis 24:33). From this we can learn a lesson; the business of the Lord demands priority over hunger and any other circumstances in our life.

Our most important task is to do the will of the Father (John 4:32,34). In John 12:25,26 we are instructed not to love our human life and day-to-day routines more than we love God. We are to serve Christ, follow Him and give up mere human desires for God's plan for our life.

Thus, when we become Christ's servant, He is always with us. By serving Christ we honor God. We see that the servant honored Abraham's God by serving Him first; then he refreshed his body with the food which had been set before him.

The Servant Requests the Hand of Rebekah for Isaac Genesis 24:34-49

The servant told Rebekah's father and family about Abraham whom they had not seen for many years. This must have been a most interesting discussion for the family that had been left behind in Mesopotamia when Abraham followed God to Canaan. He told them about Sarah and the child of faith, Isaac. He also told them the reason for his coming, and just why he had chosen Rebekah to be the wife for Isaac. After completing the whole story, he asked the family to decide

79

whether they would let Rebekah make the journey back to Canaan with him to be Isaac's wife.

Rebekah Chooses to Go with Abraham's Servant and Become the Wife of Isaac
Genesis 24:50-67

Rebekah's brother, Laban, and father, Bethuel, responded, "The thing comes from the Lord; we cannot speak to you bad or good" (Genesis 24:50) and told the servant to take Rebekah as a wife for Isaac. God had worked through circumstances to show them His plan, so they had peace. Their sister and daughter would be going to a far country where they might never see her again. Yet we see the under-girding peace that they had in knowing God's will for her.

Do you have this same kind of peace when God calls a child, relative, or friend to some far off place for mission work or some other type of work that is in His plan? God is waiting and wants to give you this peace. Will you ask Him for this today?

Abraham's servant thanked the Lord again after Laban and Bethuel gave their consent. The servant then gave more silver and gold and beautiful clothing to Rebekah. He also gave costly ornaments to her brother and to her mother (Genesis 24:52,53). When the ceremony of the giving of the gifts had been completed, everyone ate dinner and retired for the night.

In the morning the servant asked the family to send him back immediately to Abraham. Rebekah's mother and brother asked if he would be willing to let her remain with them for at least 10 days and then they would send her on to him. The custom was that the bride-to-be could wait a considerable length of time, up to a year, before she went to be a man's wife. This would be like our engagement period today.

The servant knew that this was not God's plan for Rebekah and said, "Do not delay me, since the Lord has prospered my way; let me go that I may go to my master" (Genesis 24:56). He undoubtedly knew that Isaac needed the love and comfort of a wife after his mother's death (Genesis 23:2).

The final decision was up to Rebekah. Her family said, "We will call the maiden, and ask her" (Genesis 24:57). They said to her, "Will you go with this man?"

She said, "I will go" (Genesis 24:58).

After they had all wished her joy, happiness and blessing, they sent Rebekah, accompanied by her maid and her nurse, to Canaan with Abraham's servant and his men.

We see Rebekah's faith in God's plan for her life as she chose to go

80

with the servant. As an evidence of her faith, Rebekah mounted her camel and started out on the journey of about 400 miles from Nahor to Canaan where she would become the bride of a complete stranger in a foreign land. Camels travel about three miles an hour, and one gets very hot and dirty riding them. Rebekah had a lot of time to ponder the things that she had been told about Isaac. The bracelets on her arms reminded her that she was going to marry him.

Isaac had been waiting a long time for the servant's return. At last one evening while he was out meditating in the fields at sunset, he saw the camels coming! The Hebrew word *suah* usually translated "meditate" has the meaning "walk about, pray, lament, or moan." From the usage of this word we are reminded that Isaac needed comforting (Genesis 24:63). God had sent him Rebekah to become his wife, to love and comfort him. *What is your present heartache that is causing you to lament? Are you praying about it as Isaac was praying in the field?* Won't you lift your eyes expecting God to send you comfort in some way?

At the same time that Isaac saw the camels, Rebekah lifted her eyes and saw him in the field (Genesis 24:64). She got down from her camel in respect for Isaac, the customary response to a man of his position. She quickly adjusted her veil. It was not proper for a woman to appear unveiled before her husband before the marriage had been consummated. Only then could her husband look upon her face.

The Scriptures tell us that Isaac was told all the details of the journey by the servant (Genesis 24:66). How they must have rejoiced and thanked God again for His answer to prayer. Then Isaac took Rebekah to his mother's tent and she became his wife. He loved her and Isaac was comforted after his mother's death.

This beautiful love story is more than a story because it actually happened. The Spirit of God has recorded it for us so that we can better understand God's love for us, the Church, who are said to be the Bride of Christ. In Isaac's marriage we see a portrayal of the joy and comfort that the Church (those who receive the Lord Jesus Christ by faith) has when she becomes the Bride of Christ (Ephesians 5:25-32; Revelation 21:2,9). The tremendous comfort and joy in knowing the love of Jesus Christ and His forgiveness of sins can be compared to the comfort, joy and love which Rebekah brought to Isaac.

Have you ever come to the point in your life where you have responded to the Holy Spirit's message and received Jesus Christ into your heart and life? (Revelation 3:20). God is waiting to give you comfort and love through Jesus Christ! If you have received this comfort and love, are you sharing this love and joy with others in various ways?

Study Questions

Before you begin your study this week:
1. Pray and ask God to speak to you through His Holy Spirit each day.
2. Use only your Bible for your answers.
3. Write your answers and the verses you have used.
4. Challenge questions are for those who have the time and wish to do them.
5. Personal questions are to be shared with your study group only if you wish to share.
6. As you study look for a verse to memorize this week. Write it down, carry it with you, tack it to your bulletin board, tape it to the dashboard of your car. Make a real effort to learn the verse and its reference.

FIRST DAY: Read all of the preceding notes and look up all of the Scriptures.

1. What was a helpful or new thought from the overview of Genesis 24?

2. What personal application did you select to apply to your own life?

SECOND DAY: Read Genesis 25, concentrating on verses 1-18.

1. Before Abraham died what did he give to Isaac, his son "in the faith" by Sarah?

2 a. What did he give his sons born to him by Keturah?

   b. Where were these sons sent by Abraham?

3. How old was Abraham when he died and where was he buried?

4 a. Compare Genesis 24:1 with Genesis 25:11. After Abraham's death, what did Isaac receive from God which Abraham had also received from God?

b. Where did Isaac go to live after Abraham's death?

c. At what previous time was Isaac at this place? See Genesis 24:62-67.

5. How many sons did Ishmael have and where did they live?

6. **Challenge:** God has promised to bless those who love His Son, the Lord Jesus, just as He chose to bless Abraham and Isaac many years ago. Put the following verses into your own words concerning the ways in which God blesses the Christian believer.

2 Corinthians 9:8

Ephesians 3:20 with Philippians 2:13

THIRD DAY: Read Genesis 25:19-34.

1. What did Isaac take to the Lord in prayer, and how did God answer him?

2. Rebekah also went to the Lord in prayer. Why?

3. What did the Lord tell Rebekah about the twins she would give birth to?

4. **Challenge:** God longs to have us come to Him by way of prayer today just as Isaac and Rebekah did. What do you learn about prayer from the following verses? Try to put the thoughts into your own words.

Matthew 7:7-11

John 15:7

John 16:23

5. Describe what you discover about Jacob and Esau in Genesis 25:23-28.

a. Esau

b. Jacob

6. Did Esau value his birthright as the first son? What did he do with his birthright?

FOURTH DAY: Read all of Genesis 26, concentrating on verses 1-6.

1 a. What problem arose in Canaan which had also occurred during Abraham's lifetime there?

   b. Where did Isaac go to live?

2 a. What did God tell Isaac in Genesis 26:2?

   b. What did God promise Isaac if he would stay in Canaan?

3. (Personal) Isaac lived in a land in which there was a problem (Genesis 26:1). What problem do you have right now? What part of God's promise to Isaac would you like to have God promise you today?

4. Challenge: God speaks to us through His written Word, the Bible, today. In it we find that the Lord Jesus Christ made the same promise to Christians. Explain in your own words what the following verses say concerning this.

Hebrews 13:5,6

John 14:16,17

Romans 8:37-39

5 a. What was Abraham's heart attitude which resulted in God's blessings? See Genesis 26:3-5.

b. What does this suggest about your heart attitude toward God if you want to experience His blessings in your life?

6. Did Isaac obey God, too?

FIFTH DAY: Read Genesis 26:7-22.

1. What sad thing did Isaac do which showed the same lack of trust in God for his safety which his father also did years before? Compare Genesis 20:2 and Genesis 26:6,7.

2. Isaac was a godly man who as a general rule obeyed and trusted God. How did this act in Genesis 26:7 show the truth of Romans 3:23?

3. What would Genesis 26:12 indicate that the shepherd, Isaac, became while living in Gerar? Did God bless him in this occupation?

4 a. How did the Philistines feel about Isaac and why? See Genesis 26:14.

b. What did Abimelech tell Isaac to do?

5 a. When the Philistines took away the first two wells Isaac reopened in this area, what was his reaction?

b. How did Isaac's attitude of trust in the Lord tie in with what David told the giant Philistine before he slew him with a stone? See 1 Samuel 17:47.

6. (Personal) Isaac revealed a quiet trust in God by this test of each well being taken from him. If you are in a difficult situation right now, will you *quietly trust God* in this same way to work out whatever your problem is? What does Psalm 37:5 say *concerning this?*

SIXTH DAY: Read Genesis 26:23-35.

1 a. Where did Isaac go next? Find this on your Bible map, if possible.

b. What did God promise Isaac in this place?

c. (Personal) Is there some portion of this promise that you would like to claim for your life today? Write out your thoughts as a token of your trust in God in your situation.

2. What was Isaac's response to God's promise?

3. Because Isaac trusted God in the disagreement over the wells (Genesis 26:18-22), King Abimelech and the Philistines were impressed by his attitudes and actions in the trouble. What phrase does the king use concerning Isaac that you would like to have your enemies use concerning you?

4. What did the Lord Jesus tell us we should do for our enemies? See Matthew 5:43-45.

5. **Challenge:** It may seem impossible for a person to treat his enemies this way, but the Lord Jesus has promised the Christian the power of the Holy Spirit for just such occasions. How does 1 Corinthians 2:4 encourage you concerning this power of the Holy Spirit?

6 a. How did Esau sadly disappoint his father, Isaac, and his mother, Rebekah, in Genesis 26?

  b. Which verse from this week's lesson did you choose to memorize? Why did you choose it?

THE LORD ALWAYS ANSWERS PRAYER IN TIME

Genesis 25-26

Study Notes

Abraham's Other Descendants Genesis 25:1-6

Abraham had six sons by another wife named Keturah (Genesis 25:1,2). After the birth of these sons, Abraham made Isaac his sole heir (Genesis 25:5). Abraham gave everything that God had given him to Isaac. This included the promise of the land of Canaan, the making of a great nation and the birth of the Messiah through his family line. This promise was originally given in Genesis 12:1-7, and was repeated several times by the Lord to Abraham (Genesis 13:14-17; 15:17,18; 21:12; 22:16-18). Though Abraham did not live to see God fulfill all His promises, he believed that Isaac would see them come to pass. Abraham made Isaac the heir of his covenant with God.

Abraham did not forget his other sons, for we see in Genesis 25:6 that he gave gifts to them. Then Abraham wisely sent them to a distant place in the east country so that they would not attempt to divide Isaac's inheritance with him. Note that he did this while he was still living so that everything would be left in order before he went to be with God forever. *A wise policy for us is to do what we can while we are living concerning our estates and children. After careful prayer, asking God for guidance, a Christian should get his estate in order and make preparations for his heirs before his death.*

Abraham's Death Genesis 25:7-10

Abraham lived to the good old age of 175 years. He was 100 years old when Isaac was born (Genesis 21:5; 25:20) and had lived 35 years after Isaac's marriage to Rebekah (Genesis 25:7). *When the Lord gives us eternal life He enables us to live on earth in a better and happier way than do those who are without the Lord. A promise is attached to the commandments given in Exodus 20:12, "that thy days may be long upon the land which the Lord thy God giveth thee." The Christian can find true fulfillment in life when the principles of God found in the Scriptures are applied and used daily.*

Do you spend time daily with your Lord and Savior Jesus Christ in prayer and in reading the Bible in order to allow Him to guide your life? (Psalm 91:15,16) Because Abraham's life had been filled with God, he was rewarded with a long life.

Isaac and Ishmael buried Abraham in the cave of Machpelah, in the field of Ephron. This was the field which Abraham had purchased from the Hittites in which to bury Sarah, his wife (Genesis 23:16-20). This is the last time the Scriptures record these two halfbrothers together. Since that time, the descendants of Ishmael have been against the descendants of Isaac. Even today the Arabs fight the Jewish race in the land of Abraham.

God Blesses Isaac Genesis 25:11

We read in Genesis 25:11, "after the death of Abraham God blessed Isaac his son." In Genesis 24:1 we had read that Abraham was blessed by God, and now we read that his son was also blessed by God. God has also promised to bless those who love His Son, the Lord Jesus Christ.

Just as He blessed Abraham and Isaac many years ago, He is longing to bless you when you put your trust in His Son. "Now glory be to God who by his mighty power at work within us is able to do far more than we would ever dare to ask or even dream of—infinitely beyond our highest prayers, desires, thoughts or hopes" (Ephesians 3:20).

Have you ever come to the Lord Jesus Christ in simple faith asking Him to enter into your life and be your Savior and Lord (Revelation 3:20; John 3:16,17)? If you are a Christian, have you thanked God for the wonderful ways in which He has blessed your life?

The Generations of Ishmael Genesis 25:12-18

Abraham's son Ishmael, whose mother had been Sarah's maid, Hagar, had many descendants. The 12 sons of Ishmael, grandsons of Abraham, became a great nation as God had promised their grandmother, Hagar (Genesis 16:7-14; 17:20). Undoubtedly God recorded the lineage of Ishmael to show us that He was keeping His promise to Ishmael.

Ishmael lived to be 137 years old according to Genesis 25:17. His sons lived from Havilah to Shur, which is opposite Egypt in the direction of Assyria. It was in this region that the angel of the Lord found Hagar when she fled from Sarah in Genesis 16:7-14.

The Birth of Jacob and Esau Genesis 25:19-26

Isaac was 40 years old when he married Rebekah. Isaac prayed to the Lord for his wife because she was barren. They had been married 20 years before the twins were born, so Isaac was 60 years old when Rebekah gave birth to them (Genesis 25:26). Isaac had prayed 20 long years for a son, and now his wife had given birth to two!

If we willingly continue in prayer as Isaac did, we will find at last that we did not seek in vain. God longs to have us come to Him by way of prayer today, just as Isaac and Rebekah did long ago. We are to ask, seek, and knock—just as a man gives his son the best gift he can, so our heavenly Father gives us the very best for us (Matthew 7:7-11)! As the Christian lives according to God's directions in the Scriptures and does the things that are pleasing in His eyes, the Lord then grants his or her prayers.

Carefully consider these conditions for prayer. Ask yourself if you are meeting God's requirements for answered prayer in your life today. *Remember also that God does all things on time.*

After years of waiting and seeing the fruitfulness of his half brother, Ishmael, in producing many sons (Genesis 25:12-15), Isaac was now seeing God's blessing on his own life. When he came to the end of his own resources and humbled himself before God in prayer, God in His time gave him sons. Are you willing to pray, "Lord, I know that you do all things on time! I am willing to wait for your time in answering my prayer."

In Genesis 25:22 we find that Rebekah, Isaac's wife, went to the Lord in prayer because the two children within her struggled so. What happened within the womb of Rebekah also happens within the heart of each person who comes to Jesus Christ in faith believing that He is God's Son and Savior. *No sooner is Christ invited into the life of the person than a conflict begins between the presence of the Holy Spirit in the new Christian and the opposition of the flesh, the old self.*

The apostle Paul had this struggle. The Holy Spirit led him to relate this dilemma in Romans 7:24 and 25, "So you see how it is: my new life tells me to do right, but the old nature that is still inside me

91

loves to sin. Oh, what a terrible predicament I'm in! Who will free me from my slavery to this deadly lower nature? Thank God! It has been done by Jesus Christ our Lord." Paul goes on to explain how the Holy Spirit enables the Christian to overcome sin in Romans 8:1-4.

The information that God gave to Rebekah upon her prayer to Him was an amazing revelation. "Two nations are in your womb" (Genesis 25:23). She was not only pregnant with two children, but two entirely different nations would descend from these two sons. She was told that the elder would serve the younger. The domination of Israel over Edom originates here. Edom, the elder, was subjugated by David the younger (2 Samuel 8).

When the twins were born, there was a great difference between them, and this served to confirm what God had foretold in Genesis 25:23. Esau was born red with a hairy mantle covering his body. Jacob was not. Identical twins are strikingly alike in their thoughts, dispositions and physical appearance, but these twins proved to be different in almost every way.

Jacob reached out and took hold of Esau's heel as he was born (Genesis 25:26). Heel in Hebrew is *akob*. The baby received this name with the addition of the smaller letter in the Hebrew alphabet, which is also the first letter in the name Jehovah. It was pronounced "Hakab" and showed from the beginning that he would reach out and lay hold on many things. Indeed, this would become a characteristic of Jacob. Through the discipline of God he learned the folly of some of his schemes, nevertheless he was blessed in all that he did. *At first he grasped in the flesh, but eventually he grasped the things which the Lord had for him.* In time, this baby became Israel, a prince who had "power with God" (Genesis 32:28).

Esau Sells His Birthright to Jacob
Genesis 25:27-34

We discover in Genesis 25:27 that Esau was a man of this world. He enjoyed sports; recreation seemed to be his business. He was a skilled hunter, which indicated that he devoted his time to the art of it. Apparently he never cared for being indoors, but was a man of the field, happiest when he was out in pursuit of game.

In this same verse Jacob is portrayed as an entirely different type of man. He is described as a plain and quiet man. The word "plain" is found 13 times in the Bible. It is translated as "perfect" nine times, "undefiled" twice, "upright" once and simply as "plain" once. It is the word by which God described Job (Job 1:1-8; 2:3). Jacob, like his father, was a tent dweller. He too was a pilgrim and stranger in the land, in the outdoors.

The difference between the two boys caused conflicting emotions in the parents and brought much grief to everyone (Genesis 25:28). Yes, there was favoritism in Isaac's home. The father admired and loved the older son, Esau, for he was a hunter and a hail fellow. Jacob was the idol of his mother's heart.

This situation made jealousy and strife between the two boys as well as the parents. Each tried to take advantage of the other. This unpleasantness made Esau unhappy and tempted him to give up the lasting and future blessings for immediate pleasures.

How did this temptation come to Esau? It came through a proposal his brother, Jacob, made when he was savagely hungry after a long hunting trip. Esau used the same expression we often use today when we feel so hungry that we are tormented. "I am about to die" (Genesis 25:32).

Jacob proposed that his brother should sell him his birthright for a dish of stew. It is difficult to be wise when we are hungry. *The temptation was strong. He exchanged a lasting joy for a brief gratification of appetite.*

Unrestrained passions are like the white ants of Africa that will burrow into and eat out the insides of tables and chairs, leaving the shell intact until the least pressure causes them to crumble. This sudden temptation that came to Esau was like the touch on an ant-eaten table. That he yielded to the temptation showed that for many years he had been doing nothing to discipline his desires and appetite. Esau's example should be a lesson to any Christian today. Do you value earthly things more than eternal treasures and blessings from God? *"Wherever your treasure is, there your heart and thoughts will also be"* (Luke 12:34).

Why did it make such a difference that Esau should sell the birthright? That birthright was his privilege as the first-born son. It meant that he was to receive the great promises God had made to Abraham and Isaac: (1) the founder of a holy nation; (2) through him all the nations of the earth would be blessed with the Messiah.

Undoubtedly, Jacob's mother had told him about the prophecy (Genesis 25:23) that the elder would serve the younger. He had thought of it so much that he could not wait until God's own time for it to be fulfilled. His sly proposal reveals a crafty nature. Are you willing to wait for God's own time to fulfill His blessing for you, rather than choose a crafty method such as Jacob did?

If Jacob had not taken advantage of his brother's weakness, could he have received his birthright? Certainly! If God meant for Jacob to have it, God would have found a way to give it to him.

It is never necessary to do evil that good may come. This impatience in trying to get God's blessing before God's time was also shown

93

when Abraham had a child by Sarah's handmaiden, Hagar. We saw the result of that sin. We can be sure that Jacob will reap what he sowed.

In Genesis 25:23 we see that God's promise about the future was more to Jacob than to Esau. It concerned the nations of which they were to be the fathers. Through the line of Jacob would the Messiah, the Lord Jesus Christ, come.

And what about Esau in this situation? In Genesis 25:30 he said, "Feed me . . . with that same red pottage; for I am faint." Esau, the man of the world, came back faint because nothing in the world could satisfy him.

We see many things in the world today which cause people to say, "I must have this or that or I will die." People long for power, money, a beautiful home, a good-looking husband or wife, a youthful appearance, many friends, the biggest boat, the nicest beach home, the largest car, and so on. The list could go on and on. **Have you been caught in the trap of our society? Remember that worldly enjoyment will stand us in no stead in the dying hour.**

Surely, if Esau was hungry and faint, he could have gotten a meal without the expense of his birthright. But he would not deny himself the immediate satisfaction of his appetite. Esau was careless and motivated by animal appetites and thought more about his stomach than God's blessing.

What about you? Are you careless, thinking more about your short pilgrimage on this earth than you do about God's blessing that He has promised to you as a Christian? The gratifying of sensual appetites is what ruins thousands of precious souls.

God has promised, "If we confess our sins, he is faithful and just to forgive us our sins, and to cleanse us from all unrighteousness" (1 John 1:9). Look into your own heart and see if this is the time when you should stop and ask God's forgiveness for some unruly appetite in your life today.

Esau's reasoning was very weak and we see this same reasoning used today. "Behold, I am at the point to die" (Genesis 25:32). He was foolish to believe that nothing could keep him alive except this particular stew! Surely Isaac was not so poor, nor Rebekah such a bad housekeeper that there would not have been food supplied to him

94

conveniently when he returned from the hunt! But nothing pleased him except this red pottage!

And yet, we see many things in the world today which cause people to say, "I must have this or that or I will die." People long for power, money, a beautiful home, a good-looking husband or wife, a youthful appearance, many friends, the biggest boat, the nicest beach home, the largest car, and so on. The list could go on and on!

Have you been caught in the trap of our society? Remember that worldly enjoyment will stand us in no stead in the dying hour. "My life is no longer than my hand! My whole lifetime is but a moment to you. Proud man! Frail as a breath! A shadow! And all his busy rushing ends in nothing. He heaps up riches for someone else to spend. And so Lord, my only hope is in you. Save me from being overpowered by my sins, for even fools will mock me then" (Psalm 39:5-8).

Is this your prayer today?

The Covenant Is Confirmed to Isaac
Genesis 26:1-5

Because of a famine in the land of Canaan, Isaac went to live temporarily in the land of the Philistines (Genesis 26:1). Isaac had been trained to believe that the land of Canaan had been granted to him and to his heirs, but now there is a famine in Canaan. What should he think of the promise when the Promised Land would not provide bread for his family? Isaac clung to God's promise regardless of the circumstances. *We are not to look at our circumstances, but at God's promises.*

The king Abimelech spoken of in this verse is not the king of the Philistines whom Abraham knew. The name was probably not a proper name, but like "Pharaoh" a title for the ruler of the Philistines. Abimelech means "the king, my father."

While Isaac was in Gerar the Lord appeared to him and said, "Do not go down to Egypt" (Genesis 26:2). The Lord told Isaac to stay in the land of the Philistines and promised that He would be with him and bless him and his descendants. He again promised Isaac as He had promised Abraham, "I will give [you] all these lands, and I will fulfill the oath which I swore to Abraham your father" (Genesis 26:3). God also promised to multiply Isaac's descendants as the stars of heaven and to give his descendants all these lands.

Again He promised that through the family of Abraham and Isaac and their descendants all the nations of the earth shall be blessed. This promise refers to the coming of the Lord Jesus Christ, the Messiah, through the family line. God said He would do these things because

"Abraham obeyed my voice and kept my charge, my commandments, my statutes, and my laws" (26:5).

Do you need God's blessing? Do you have problems today just as Isaac had the problem of a famine? Why not claim Philippians 4:19 for your life today? Yes, God will supply all of your needs according to His riches in glory! *Will you believe and receive these wonderful promises which God has for you today?*

Fearful Isaac Deceives Abimelech
Genesis 26:6-11

We see here the weak, human side of Isaac in his fear of Abimelech—a fear that caused him to lie about his wife, Rebekah. Because Rebekah was beautiful, Isaac was afraid the king would kill him so that he, the king, could take her as his wife. In fearing for his life, Isaac momentarily failed to trust God, the One who had promised to bless him.

How often we fall into this same trap! We need to go to the Lord and confess our sin of unbelief in His promises to us (1 John 1:9).

One day Abimelech looked out of his window and saw Isaac "sporting" (caressing) his wife. So Abimelech called Isaac and confronted him with the fact that he knew that Rebekah was his wife rather than his sister. Abimelech rebuked Isaac for this deception. A high moral code must have existed in the kingdom at this time. The king warned all of the people saying, "Whoever touches this man or his wife shall be put to death" (Genesis 26:11).

The Lord Blesses Isaac in Gerar
Genesis 26:12-14

Isaac had taken with him many servants, flocks of sheep, herds of cattle, camels and donkeys. He had pitched his tents in the land of the Philistines, he reaped great harvests, a hundredfold (Genesis 26:12). Isaac was not only a herdsman and a shepherd but now was becoming an agriculturist. For every bushel of seed he planted, he got a hundred bushels of grain.

Isaac's Troubles over the Wells
Genesis 26:14-22

The Philistines began to fear Isaac and to envy him when they saw how great and how wealthy he was becoming. They envied him because of the number of his sheep, cattle, servants and wells. In their resentment of him, they even stopped up his wells by filling them with earth (26:15). These wells had not been dug by the Philistines, but by the servants of Isaac's father, Abraham.

Because of his people's increasing jealousy of Isaac, Abimelech, their king, said to Isaac, "Go somewhere else . . . for you have become too rich and powerful for us" (26:16).

So Isaac started back to his own country and camped in the valley of Gerar. In this part of the land of the Philistines Isaac's father, Abraham, had lived many years before. Abraham had also dug wells here in the places where he had camped so that he would have water for his animals and his household.

In a country that is dry most of the year, as was this land, wells are necessary even though to dig and wall up the wells takes much time and a great amount of hard work. Because his father had dug these wells at Gerar, they belonged to Isaac. So Isaac cleaned out the wells that the Philistines had filled up with earth after Abraham had died.

The Philistines were both quarrelsome and dishonest. They fought with Isaac's herdsmen and said, "The water is ours" (26:20). The truth was that the water belonged to Isaac.

Isaac might easily have called out his soldiers to drive away these men, but instead he might have said, "I will not fight about such a matter. I have plenty of servants, and we will just dig another well. This country belongs to the Philistines. God has promised Canaan to my family. I would rather live at peace with these men than have a dozen wells." So Isaac and his servants dug another well, and each time the herdsmen of the Philistines demanded that one, too.

Instead of fighting with the Philistines for the wells that were rightfully his, Isaac did a much wiser thing. He dug new wells of water. *He chose to give up his rights to the wells rather than quarrel with his neighbors.* Do you think that was the right thing to do? Indeed it was! He showed far greater strength of character than if he had taken the easier way and fought because of the unjust way he was treated.

Isaac was not only peaceable and patient, but he had a great faith in God. He said, "The Lord hath made room for us" (Genesis 26:22). Isaac reminds us of the verse in Matthew 5:9, "Blessed are the peacemakers: for they shall be called the children of God." Are you a peacemaker? The Lord Jesus Christ wants to help you be a peacemaker!

God Blesses Isaac the Peacemaker
Genesis 26:23-35

Finally Isaac and his family returned to their own home in Beersheba. There the Lord appeared to Isaac in a dream one night and said, "I am the God of Abraham thy father: fear not, for I am with thee, and will bless thee, and multiply thy seed [their children and children's children] for my servant Abraham's sake. And he built an altar there, and called upon the name of the Lord" (Genesis 26:24,25).

God had been watching all the time and was pleased that Isaac had been a peacemaker instead of a fighter. Isaac's response to God's promise was to build an altar and to worship God. Be sure that God will notice *your* love for Him expressed by your worship of Him, and be pleased with you, just as He was pleased with Isaac at this time.

The king of the Philistines felt so ashamed that he and his friends afterwards went to Isaac and wanted him to promise to be friends. Isaac had a chance to be mean if he wanted to, but instead he made a great feast, treated them kindly and took care of them at night. The next day before they left, the king of the Philistines and Isaac made friendly promises to each other (Genesis 26:26-31).

King Abimelech and the Philistines were impressed by Isaac's attitudes and actions in the time of trouble (which was really God's testing of how Isaac would respond to Him). The king used some phrases to describe Isaac which were very complimentary. Genesis 26:28, "We saw certainly that the Lord was with thee." Genesis 26:29, "Thou art now the blessed of the Lord." Genesis 26:31, "They departed from him in peace."

Certainly we would like to have our enemies see us in the same light! Jesus Christ will help you to live in harmony with others, and to consider the feelings and needs of others before your own. His great love can control your actions so there can be peace and happiness wherever you are! Will you make yourself available today to the Giver of this great love, the Lord Jesus Christ?

Study Questions

Before you begin your study this week:
1. Pray and ask God to speak to you through His Holy Spirit each day.
2. Use only your Bible for your answers.
3. Write your answers and the verses you have used.
4. Challenge questions are for those who have the time and wish to do them.
5. Personal questions are to be shared with your study group only if you wish to share.
6. As you study look for a verse to memorize this week. Write it down, carry it with you, tack it to your bulletin board, tape it to the dashboard of your car. Make a real effort to learn the verse and its reference.

FIRST DAY: Read all of the preceding notes and look up all the Scriptures.

1. What was a helpful or new thought from the overview of Genesis 25 and 26?

2. What personal application did you select to apply to your own life?

SECOND DAY: Read all of Genesis 27, concentrating on verses 1-17.

1 a. Describe Isaac's physical state at the time he called Esau to him.

b. What did Isaac ask Esau to do and what did he promise to do for Esau after this?

2. Esau was Isaac's oldest son. What do you discover about him in the following verses?

Genesis 25:20-23

Genesis 25:27-34

3 a. Who overheard all that Isaac spoke to Esau in Genesis 27:5?

b. Rebekah undoubtedly remembered and believed what the Lord had said to her in Genesis 25:23—"The elder shall serve the younger." She knew that it was Jacob whom God wanted to receive the blessing, so what did she do by her own planning to make sure that it was Jacob, not Esau, who received Isaac's blessing?

c. How did Rebekah disguise Jacob to appear to be Esau?

4. Though Rebekah knew God wanted Jacob to be blessed, what was wrong with the way she tried to "help God"?

5 a. (Personal) Can you think of some ways in which you may have tried to "help God" accomplish His plan by *wrong methods*— rather than letting God use His perfect ways to bring about His will for your own life or someone else's life?

b. (Personal) When you find yourself in a difficult place, do you stop to pray and ask God for directions? If you have experienced such an answer to prayer, would you be willing to share this with your discussion group to encourage others?

6. **Challenge:** What do the following Scriptures teach about parental-child relationships? Put them into your own words if possible.

Ephesians 6:4

Proverbs 22:6

THIRD DAY: Read Genesis 27:18-29.

1. Did Jacob cooperate with his mother's deception in getting the blessing? What sin did he commit twice when he entered his father's room?

2. Was Jacob responsible for his deceitfulness, or do you believe his mother was the only guilty one in this episode? See Romans 3:23 to help you.

3. (Personal) At times we are tempted to blame someone else when we are "forced" to do something that we know is deceitful. Do you feel that the "end" justified the "means"? Do you believe God finds such things acceptable in His Holy presence? Does our present society condone such thinking?

4. How do the following Scriptures relate to some of the things mentioned in question 3?

Proverbs 12:22

Mark 10:19

5. **Challenge:** Briefly state what the blessing was from Genesis 27:28,29.

6. (Personal) Have you made plans this week which you have not prayed about? Why not stop right now and talk to the Lord about these plans. Ask Him to show you if they are His plans, or human engineering. Why not ask the Lord to guide you by His Holy Spirit in all that you plan and do this week? How does John 16:7,8,13,14 encourage you to pray in this way?

FOURTH DAY: Read Genesis 27:30-40.

1 a. As soon as Isaac had given the blessing to Jacob, who came in to see him?

   b. What did this person bring with him?

   c. What did he ask Isaac to do?

2. When Isaac realized he had given the blessing to someone other than his eldest son, what was his reaction?

3. **Challenge:** With this trembling (verse 33) it would seem that Isaac's desire to have his own way and bless his oldest son began to totter and fall. How does Genesis 25:28 help you to understand both Isaac and Rebekah's actions concerning the giving of the family blessing in Genesis 27?

4. (Personal) Do you ever put your own desires above what you know is God's plan for yourself, your finances, your family, your

102

friends, etc.? If we are to have the joy of the Lord in our hearts, we must have the plan of the Lord in our wills! Is your prayer, "Lord, bend me in your way. Give me joy in knowing and doing your will?"

5 a. What does Isaac say in Genesis 27:33 which indicates that he realized that it was God's will for Jacob to be blessed?

  b. What was Esau's reaction to missing the blessing? What actions and words reveal his true character in Genesis 27:34-38?

6. **Challenge:** In the Bible God promises to help us if we sincerely seek to know and do His will or plan for our lives. Express in your own words what the following verses say concerning this.

   Romans 12:1,2

   Psalm 25:5,9

FIFTH DAY: Read Genesis 27:41 through Genesis 28:4.

1 a. What does Esau feel toward Jacob and what does he plan to do to Jacob after Isaac, their father, dies?

  b. What does 1 John 3:15,16 say about hatred and love?

2. (Personal) Have you received God's love by receiving His Son Jesus Christ as your Savior and Lord? Read Revelation 3:20. How are you helping others to receive God's love?

103

3. What plan did Rebekah make for Jacob's safety when she learned of Esau's plan in Genesis 27:42?

4 a. How did Rebekah convince Isaac to send his son Jacob away at this time?

b. Rebekah said she was weary of life because of the Hittite women in Genesis 27:46. Could she have meant the Hittite wives Esau had married in Genesis 26:34,35? What were Rebekah and Isaac's emotions toward these two Hittite women?

5. Isaac sent Jacob away. What were his parting words to his son in Genesis 28:1-4?

6. **Challenge:** Christian marriage symbolizes the marriage of the believer to Jesus Christ, as a bride is joined to a bridegroom. Mixed marriage between a Christian and a non-Christian is completely foreign to the Word of God. Both Rebekah and Isaac wanted Jacob to marry a woman who worshiped the one true God. Read Ephesians 5:21-32, and record some thoughts from these verses which particularly impress you about the marriage relationship, and the relationship of Christ toward those who love Him as their Savior and Lord.

SIXTH DAY: Read Genesis 28:5-9.

1. Did Jacob obey his father?

104

2. Where did Jacob go and with whom did he live?

3. Who was Jacob to find in this place? See Genesis 28:6.

4. What did Esau learn from all this according to Genesis 28:8? Note: The Hittites were Canaanites because they lived in the land of Canaan.

5. What did Esau do next to try to please his father?

6 a. Esau was trying to please his parents by this act, but one wonders if his inward heart attitude had changed. How do the following Scriptures help you in understanding that it is our "heart response" that God desires rather than "outward acts" with no real "love" for Him?

Proverbs 21:2

Ezekiel 11:19,20

b. Which Bible verse have you chosen to hide in your heart this week?

2. Where did Jacob go to dwell when he left home?

3. Who was Isaac afraid the place Beer-sheba was ...?

4. What did Jacob hear from the LORD to him in Genesis 28:4 NIV.
That I have here came, now Jacob are those, and multitude of earth.

5. Who did the men hadn't by his son's table?

6. Because writing or take the angel ... to ...?
Is it his reason that unition the ... the ... because of eight
angel yesterday ... who are ... other's ... but ... her, then
that had that ... dream ... that of ... flower ... within
... to ...

Proverbs 3:10

3 John 1:1 NIV.

3:10. Bible ... take ... in ... ... from ... this
... week.

GOD'S WILL MUST BE DONE IN GOD'S WAY

Genesis 27—28:1-9

Study Notes

Aged Isaac Prepares to Bless Esau
Genesis 27:1-4

Isaac, father of Jacob and Esau, was 60 years old when the boys were born. By the time they were grown men, he was feeble and almost blind (Genesis 27:1). He could not tell his sons apart unless he heard their voices and felt their hands. Jacob's hands were smooth, but Esau's were rough and hairy as he was a hunter and a man of the field (Genesis 25:27,28).

Old age can be a blessing or a disappointment. Age can become a problem if you become self-willed and determined to do what you want rather than what you know God is asking you to do. With Isaac, old age started out horribly and the events of this chapter show how self-willed he had become.

Isaac is now about 137 years old, about the age of his half-brother, Ishmael, when he died (Genesis 25:17). Perhaps this is why he thought that he too would soon die. However, he recovered from his weakness and lived 43 years longer, dying at the age of 180 (Genesis 35:28).

The Bible tells us that the outward man, our physical body, perishes but the inward man is renewed day-by-day (2 Corinthians 4:16).

Our prayer needs to be, "Lord, renew me daily."

One day Isaac, now a very old man, called Esau and said, "Take your weapons, your quiver and your bow, and go out to the field, and hunt game for me, and prepare for me savory food, such as I love, and bring it to me that I may eat; that I may bless you before I die" (Genesis 27:3,4).

Here we see Isaac's self-will in his old age, for he undoubtedly remembered God's saying that the elder son, Esau, would serve the younger son, Jacob (Genesis 25:23). Yet Isaac loved Esau more than Jacob because the father could eat of the older son's game, and he enjoyed having this son who was a skillful hunter and a man of the field. So, because Isaac loved Esau more, he was determined to give the blessing of the family to him rather than to Jacob, the twin who was quiet and more thoughtful in manner.

The emphasis in this passage on food and on Isaac's love for it is an indication of the predominance of his physical appetite in his old age. Paul wrote about Christians whose god is their belly, and whose minds are on earthly things, and said that they were enemies of the cross of Christ (Philippians 3:18,19).

What about you? Is your mind on your physical needs constantly or are your thoughts centered on heavenly things and on what the Lord Jesus Christ wants you to do this day by the power of His Holy Spirit? We need to ask the Lord to help us set our affections on things above (Philippians 4:4-7).

Rebekah Takes Matters into Her Own Hands Genesis 27:5-7

Rebekah overheard Isaac talking to Esau, so she called Jacob and told him what she had overheard. The mother sets the tone of a home, and in this particular event we find that Rebekah was deceitful, proud and selfish. She wanted her way now, and was not willing for the Lord to work out His plan for Jacob's life "in the Lord's time." She showed a lack of faith in the Lord's promise. If she had been willing to wait, He would have given Jacob the birthright blessing in His time and way as He had promised her in Genesis 25:23.

Because Rebekah's "pet" was Jacob (Genesis 25:28), she immediately began to devise a clever scheme to get the birthright for her favorite son. She ordered Jacob to kill and dress two kids. She started the fire and got the water boiling so that the goat venison could be prepared to fool Isaac and to make him think that Esau had returned from the hunt and prepared the stew for his father (Genesis 27:5-10).

Rebekah thought that the pressure was on; there was no time to lose. She became a "pressure cooker"! She cooked the two kids and made them taste like venison stew. The deception was successful— but it was all wrong.

Do you ever feel like you are in a pressure cooker, and that you have to scheme and plan to make things "come out right" in your situation? Do you try to "help God" accomplish His plans by wrong methods rather than letting God use His perfect ways to bring about His will for your own life or for someone else's life?

One wonders what would have happened if Rebekah had trusted the Lord and gone to her husband Isaac and honestly reminded him of God's promise to bless Jacob. She could have gently told him of how Esau had not treasured his birthright and had sold it to Jacob for a simple stew. She could have gently reminded Isaac that Esau had disobeyed God's plan for His people by marrying two Hittite women rather than marrying those who worshiped the one true God (Genesis 26:34,35).

The Bible teaches us that if a child commits sin in obedience to his mother, God holds her responsible. The weight of judgment that will fall on such mothers is a warning to us today. **How many mothers are more interested in their children's physical graces and popularity than in their spiritual knowledge? Such priorities can only bring heartache to a mother or father.**

Parents should comprehend that the purpose of discipline is to make it easier for children to obey their heavenly Father. **A child who has learned to obey his parents will find it easier to transfer his obedience to the Lord when he turns in faith to Jesus Christ.**

Since God meant for Jacob to have the blessing, He could have brought it about without the conniving of Rebekah. The result of her hasty decision was that she would never see her favorite son again, for he had to be banished into a far country to protect his life. Reread the passage from Philippians 4:4-7. Do you see how Rebekah could have found her peace with God if she had stopped to pray and tell God her needs at this point? *Are you willing to stop and pray and tell God your needs when you are in a pressure-cooker situation?*

Rebekah and Jacob Conspire for Him to Receive Isaac's Blessing Genesis 27:8-29

Together Rebekah and Jacob planned to deceive Isaac so that Jacob instead of Esau would receive his father's blessing. Jacob would then be assured of his birthright. We see that she told Jacob, "My son, obey my word as I command you!" (Genesis 27:8) Rebekah had a "smother love" for her son, Jacob. She encouraged him to lie and to deceive by her orders.

The Bible teaches us that if a child commits sin in obedience to his mother, God holds her responsible. The weight of judgment that will fall on such mothers is a warning to us today. *How many mothers are more interested in their children's physical graces and popularity than in their spiritual knowledge? Such priorities can only bring heartache to a mother or father.*

Parents should comprehend that the purpose of discipline is to make it easier for children to obey their heavenly Father. *A child who has learned to obey his parents will find it easier to transfer his obedience to the Lord when he turns in faith to Jesus Christ.* The undisciplined child slips easily into unbelief and sin.

Why not stop and pray right now? Ask the Lord to help you to be obedient to His will today. Ask Him to teach you in His ways so that you may teach your children in His ways also. These same principles can be applied in your relationship with other people.

Jacob lied to his blind old father. Rebekah covered Jacob's hands and neck with the skins of goats. She dressed him in Esau's clothes. She gave him food that Isaac liked. So Jacob went into his father's room and pretended to be Esau. He acted a lie. Lies do not always have to be spoken. They can be acted out just as Jacob acted out his.

Do you feel that the end justifies the means, as Jacob and his mother did? Do you believe that God finds such actions acceptable in His holy Presence? *Our present society condones any actions that allow you to get ahead in the world. Never be the person who influences a friend, business associate, child, husband or wife to take such deceitful action in order to achieve gain.* As you examine your own life, now is the time to ask the Lord Jesus Christ to forgive you and to cleanse you from any deceit. Now is the time to make a new beginning with God.

Isaac asked his son to come near so he could kiss him (Genesis 27:26). Then he blessed him. This blessing was one which included first of all material blessing (Genesis 27:28) and also leadership of other nations and his brothers (Genesis 27:29). All this came to pass for Jacob, but not because Isaac laid his hands on him; God planned it

110

all that way. Jacob also experienced definite consequences of his sin. He had to flee from his home and wander for many years.

Esau Seeks Revenge Genesis 27:30-45

We find that as soon as Isaac had finished blessing Jacob, Esau, his brother, came in from hunting (Genesis 27:30). He also prepared a savory meal from the venison he had obtained. He brought it to his father and asked him to eat it so that he could bless him.

"His father Isaac said to him, 'Who are you?'"

"He answered, 'I am your son, your first born, Esau'" (27:32).

When Isaac realized that he had given his blessing to someone other than his eldest son whom he had been determined to bless, he trembled violently (Genesis 27:33).

Isaac had a wonderful record of faith surrendered to God (Genesis 22). He was submissive to God in faith regarding his marriage (Genesis 24). Then in Genesis 26:25 we see Isaac persevering in his faith as he "built an altar there and called upon the name of the Lord, and pitched his tent there."

Why did Isaac's spiritual life ebb as he grew older? Was it because he had a love of ease and enjoyed having his favorite son pamper him by bringing him good food? Did he have his eyes placed on these earthly pleasures and ignored the heavenly blessings which God had so faithfully given him through the years?

With this trembling which Isaac displayed in Genesis 27:33, it would seem that Isaac's desire to have his own way and to bless his oldest son began to totter and fall. His trembling seems to indicate that he recognized his lack of faith in this matter and his disobedience to God. Perhaps he began to realize that he had put the love of his favorite son above God's will and plan for the blessing. From reading this passage, it seems as though Isaac willfully planned to bless Esau without talking the matter over with Rebekah.

Rebekah, too, had grown weak in her faith in her old age as we note by her devious plotting to fool her husband Isaac. *But not just Isaac and Rebekah sinned. We see sin in Esau's selfish desires and sin in Jacob's cooperation in the deception.*

And if we really look honestly into our own hearts, we see that we, too, have sinned and come short of the glory of God. Many a time we have rebelled against God's perfect plan for us and tried to arrange the circumstances just as Rebekah and Jacob did. Many times we have determined to do what we want to do rather than what God has planned for our lives and for our loved ones, just as Isaac determined to bless the son that he wanted to bless.

But there is an answer in the Scriptures for all of us. Romans

3:24,25, "Yet now God declares us 'not guilty' of offending him if we trust in Jesus Christ, who in his kindness freely takes away our sins. For God sent Christ Jesus to take the punishment for our sins and to end all God's anger against us. He used Christ's blood and our faith as the means of saving us from his wrath."

If you desire the Lord Jesus Christ's forgiveness, put your name into Romans 3:24,25, in place of the word "us." Claim for yourself the forgiveness of the Lord Jesus Christ by faith.

What was Esau's reaction? "He cried out with an exceedingly great and bitter cry," and demanded some form of blessing from his father (Genesis 27:34). In Genesis 27:34-38 we find Esau's real character revealed to us. He cried out and was bitter, yet he had sold his birthright for a mess of pottage in Genesis 25:27-34! Esau was also a liar, for he said that his brother had taken his birthright from him. Rather, Esau himself sold his birthright of his own free will. Esau lifted up his voice and wept and acted like a child rather than a man under these circumstances. Thus we see in Esau bitterness, selfishness, lying and failure to face the fact of his own lack of character. *He was not yielded to God's plan.*

God has promised to bless us if we will yield to His plan for our lives. In John 4:34 we read that Jesus' greatest desire was to do the will of God and to finish His work. In Romans 12:1,2 the Christian is taught to present his body a living sacrifice and not be conformed to the will of society and what others think we should do.

We are to let God renew our minds so that we may know and do what is the good and perfect and acceptable will of God! We are to pray as the Psalmist did in Psalm 25:5 and 9, "Lead me in thy truth, and teach me: for thou art the God of my salvation; on thee do I wait all the day . . . The meek will he guide in judgment: and the meek will he teach his way." Will you pray this prayer from Psalm 25 today for your life?

We also see revenge and hatred in Esau's character as he plots to kill his brother Jacob. "The days of mourning for my father are approaching; then I will kill my brother Jacob" (Genesis 27:41). Esau knew his father hadn't long to live and he was already plotting how to seek his revenge on Jacob.

Revenge has never solved a problem in this world. It will not solve any problem which you may face today. Revenge on Esau's part showed his lack of faith in God to take care of him no matter what the circumstances were. Those who seek revenge today show this same lack of faith in God to take care of them in their circumstances.

Is revenge a part of your life? It is forbidden by God in His Word. "Say not, I will do so to him as he hath done to me: I will render to the man according to his work" (Proverbs 24:29).

112

The Lord Jesus Christ Himself was the perfect example of how to react in a situation where a person feels wrongly treated. "This suffering is all part of the work God has given you. Christ, who suffered for you, is your example. Follow in his steps: He never sinned, never told a lie, never answered back when insulted; when he suffered he did not threaten to get even; he left his case in the hands of God who always judges fairly" (1 Peter 2:21-23).

Will you let the Lord Jesus deal with any feelings of revenge in your life today? Will you follow the pattern that He set for you? Are you willing to pray, "Lord, forgive me and deal with my root of rebellion and revenge today."

God promises to forgive us and to cleanse us from all sin when we pray a prayer of confession like this to Him (1 John 1:9). *God would have forgiven Esau if Esau had only come to Him and humbled himself before God.*

Rebekah heard about Esau's terrible plan to kill Jacob and so she sent for her son and made a plan for him to escape (Genesis 27:42-45). She suggested that he go to her brother Laban's home in Haran. She told Jacob to stay there until Esau's anger had quieted down and then she promised she would send for Jacob when it was safe for him to return.

What sorrow had been brought upon this whole family because of their rejection of God's perfect plan for each one of their lives. Isaac and Rebekah had to let their younger son leave home. Rebekah would never see him again because she would die before Jacob returned home again.

The chain reaction of sin now becomes evident. Rebekah must reap the harvest of the seed which she had sown. If she had trusted and obeyed, her favorite son would have received the birthright and stayed with her. Now he had to flee to a place foreign to him.

There is a great truth here for our lives. *If we grasp at things selfishly and willfully outside of God's plan, no matter how well we succeed we shall never be satisfied.* When our desires are apart from God's perfect plan He cannot give us the desires of our heart.

Proverbs 21:2 tells us "Every way of a man is right in his own eyes: but the Lord pondereth the hearts." God has promised when we come to Him, He will take away our stony hearts and put a new spirit within us. He will give us hearts of flesh and we will be eager to walk in His ways and do them. And then we shall be God's people, and He shall be our God (Ezekiel 11:19,20).

Only through inviting the Lord Jesus Christ into our lives as our Savior and Lord can God take away our stony hearts and put into us hearts of flesh today. "Whoever denies the Son does not have the Father either; he who acknowledges the Son has the Father also" (1

113

John 2:23). Do you have the Father because you have acknowledged His Son the Lord Jesus Christ and invited Him into your life to be your Savior and Lord? How are you helping others in this area?

Isaac Sends Jacob to Laban
Genesis 27:46—Genesis 28:1-9

Rebekah convinced Isaac to send their son, Jacob, away. She told him that she did not want Jacob to marry one of the Hittite women of the land as Esau had done in Genesis 26:34,35. She told Isaac that "I am weary of my life because of the Hittite women. If Jacob marries one of the Hittite women such as these, one of the women of the land, what good will my life be to me?" (Genesis 27:46)

We read in Genesis 26:34,35 that both Isaac and Rebekah were bitter when Esau took two wives from among the Hittite people. The Hittites were the people who were living in the land of Canaan at this time and who did not worship the One true living God.

Isaac agreed to send Jacob away and his parting words are recorded in Genesis 28:1-4. He instructed Jacob not to take a wife of the daughters of Canaan. The purpose was that the line of Christ must not be mixed with the line of unbelievers. Isaac instructed Jacob to take a wife from one of the daughters of Rebekah's brother, Laban (Genesis 28:2). He then blessed Jacob by saying, "God Almighty bless you and make you fruitful and multiply you, so that you may become a company of peoples. May he give the blessing of Abraham to you and to your descendants with you, that you may take possession of the land of your sojournings which God gave to Abraham!" (Genesis 28:3,4) *If only Isaac had called Jacob in the first place, all of this trouble could have been avoided. In Genesis 28:1-4 it seems that Isaac has at last surrendered to the will of God.*

Jacob consented at once to leave home to seek a wife as his father directed him to do. Deep down in his heart Jacob had a spiritual stature that came forth at this time. He wanted God's blessing and the birthright which included a double portion of the father's inheritance (Deuteronomy 21:17) and authority in the place of the father in the family (Genesis 27:29). The birthright also included the title to the land of promise. This title meant future possession of the actual land of Canaan which God had promised to Abraham in the covenant He made with him. And perhaps the most exciting part of the birthright was that the Savior of mankind would come through Abraham's descendants. Thus the Savior of mankind would come through the descendants of Jacob also.

Perhaps you have never thought about a spiritual birthright and yet you, too, have one. Perhaps you have been born into a Christian

114

family where you learned God's Word from the moment you were old enough to hear and understand it. You may be from a home where you read the Bible and prayed together. You have been taught to read your Bible, to pray alone and to listen to God's voice speak to you by the Holy Spirit through His Word. This is a great inheritance.

Yet there is a greater spiritual birthright which each one of us has whether we were born into a Christian home or not, and that is the opportunity to know the Lord Jesus Christ as our Savior and Lord. Today, we can hear Him knocking (Revelation 3:20) as we hear God's Word spoken to us in churches, over radio, through television, through great meetings and in Bible study groups such as in Joy of Living. You have the birthright to receive eternal life through faith in the Lord Jesus Christ who died and rose again for your sins.

Read carefully these words which describe the birthright which is being offered to you. "Because of his kindness you have been saved through trusting Christ. And even trusting is not of yourselves; it too is a gift from God. Salvation is not a reward for the good we have done, so none of us can take any credit for it. It is God himself who has made us what we are and given us new lives from Christ Jesus; and long ages ago he planned that we should spend these lives in helping others" (Ephesians 2:8-10).

Have you received your spiritual birthright by receiving the Lord Jesus Christ into your life as your Savior and Lord? Christ died for you and was raised again so that you might be forgiven your sins and be given a new life through Him. Have you received His new life into your being through faith? *How are you helping others to find their spiritual birthright?*

Study Questions

Before you begin your study this week:
1. Pray and ask God to speak to you through His Holy Spirit each day.
2. Use only your Bible for your answers.
3. Write your answers and the verses you have used.
4. Challenge questions are for those who have the time and wish to do them.
5. Personal questions are to be shared with your study group only if you wish to share.
6. As you study look for a verse to memorize this week. Write it down, carry it with you, tack it to your bulletin board, tape it to the dashboard of your car. Make a real effort to learn the verse and its reference.

FIRST DAY: Read all of the preceding notes and look up all of the Scriptures.

1. What was a helpful or new thought from the overview of Genesis 27 and the first part of Genesis 28?

2. What personal application did you select to apply to your own life?

SECOND DAY: Read Genesis 28:10-14.

1 a. What kind of accommodations did Jacob have on the first night of his journey from Beer-sheba to Haran?

   b. What did Jacob see ascending and descending on the ladder in his dream?

   c. What do you learn that angels are to the Christian today? Read Hebrews 1:14.

116

2. **Challenge:** Read the following Scriptures and describe how God has sent angels to help human beings.

Exodus 23:20

1 Kings 19:5,6

3. (Personal) Have the verses in question 2 given you a greater appreciation of God's loving care through ministering angels? Are these verses and thoughts completely new to you?

4. Who appeared at the top of the ladder in Jacob's dream and what did he say? Give words from Genesis 28:13,14.

5. **Challenge:** What phrase in Genesis 28:14 speaks of God's promise to Abraham (Genesis 12:3) of the birth of the Lord Jesus Christ from his family line?

6 a. Read the following verses. Write down how we have been blessed by the coming of the Lord Jesus Christ to earth as perfect God—perfect man.

John 14:6

Galatians 1:4

b. (Personal) Have you invited the Lord Jesus Christ into your life as Savior and God so that you can enjoy these blessings?

THIRD DAY: Read Genesis 28:15-21.

1. What promise did God make to Jacob in Genesis 28:15 which you can claim for your own life if you are a Christian? Try to put this

117

promise into your own words as a promise from God to you, and put your name in the verse.

2 a. What similar promise did the Lord Jesus Christ make to His disciples and to all Christians just before He ascended into heaven? See Matthew 28:20.

   b. Summarize any further thoughts on this promise of the Lord Jesus Christ that are revealed to us in Hebrews 13:5,6.

3 a. (Personal) As a Christian, are you aware that God is not only with you at this moment, but that He dwells within your body in the person of the Holy Spirit?

   b. Summarize in your own words what the Lord Jesus Christ said about the Holy Spirit (the Comforter) in John 14:16,17.

4 a. When Jacob awoke from his sleep, what did he say in Genesis 28:16? From this remark, do you think he was lonely and afraid when he laid his head on the stone pillow before his dream?

   b. (Personal) Do you have many fears for your safety, especially at night? Why not claim the parts of Genesis 28:15 and 16 which will assure you that God is with you and will keep you just as he kept Jacob? Why not underline these phrases in your Bible now? Share any victory with your discussion group that the Lord may give you through these words this week.

5 a. What did Jacob do in the morning after his dream, and what did he name the place?

b. **Challenge:** What statement did Jacob make in Genesis 28:21 which indicates that he intended to trust God as the Lord of his life from then on?

6. What statement did David make in Psalm 63:1 which is similar to Jacob's statement in Genesis 28:21?

FOURTH DAY: Read Genesis 28:22.

1. What did Jacob say he would give to God from now on?

2. From Moses to Jesus Christ the tithe was a legal obligation. What does Leviticus 27:30-32 say concerning this?

3. What wonderful promise concerning the tithe is given in Malachi 3:10?

4. Since the coming of the Lord Jesus Christ, God's people are freed from tithing as an obligation to Old Testament law. Yet it is doubtful that a truly yielded Christian will be content with giving only 10 percent to the Lord. Everything belongs to God. What do the following Scriptures in the New Testament say about giving to God? Briefly express the ideas in your own words.

Matthew 6:1-4

1 Corinthians 16:2

119

5. What other guideline for giving is mentioned in 1 John 3:17? What connection has our love of God to this kind of giving?

6 a. (Personal) Will you pray about your heart attitude concerning your gifts to God?

b. Which of the verses on tithing and giving has challenged or encouraged you the most today?

FIFTH DAY: Read Genesis 29:1-20.

1 a. With Genesis 28:10-22 in mind, read Deuteronomy 32:9-13. What does Moses record that God did for Jacob after this dream and worship experience at Bethel? Put these thoughts in your own words if possible.

b. (Personal) Which of these blessings recorded in Deuteronomy 32:9-13 do you claim for yourself as a Christian today? If you have experienced similar blessings given by God, would you share them with your discussion group to encourage others to know that God is continually blessing the Christian today?

2. When Jacob arrived in his Uncle Laban's area (the land of the people of the East), what did he see there according to Genesis 29:2,3 and what event was occurring there?

3. **Challenge:** Think of the well as symbolic and compare it to the Word of God, the Bible. Some people do not go to the Bible them-

120

selves. They wait for preachers and teachers to roll back the stone over the well and *give them* the water (Word of God). What do the following verses say concerning the Bible?

2 Timothy 3:16,17

John 20:31

4. What did Jacob do when he saw Rachel, Laban's daughter? Read Genesis 29:5-11.

5. Rebekah, Jacob's mother, was a hard worker and yet was full of joy and at peace in her work. Remember when she drew water for all of the camels of Eliezer? (Genesis 24:18,19) Her niece, Laban's daughter, was this same type of woman, as we find her watching and caring for the sheep. What a difference it makes in the home when women understand that the Lord is pleased if they are faithful homemakers. Read Proverbs 31:10-31 and put down three or four thoughts that impress you the most concerning a good woman. Be sure and give the verse with each thought.

6. What was Laban's response to Jacob's arrival, and what kind of wages did Jacob ask of him? Read Genesis 29:13-20.

SIXTH DAY: Read Genesis 29:21-35.

1. How did Laban trick Jacob concerning the wife he promised him after seven years of work? What reason did he give for his actions? Give verses.

2. What did Jacob have to do for Laban so that he could have Rachel for his wife?

3. Describe in your own words what you learn about Rachel and Leah from the following verses.

   Genesis 29:17

   Genesis 29:30

   Genesis 29:31

4. Did Leah recognize that the Lord had seen her situation? Yes! You can tell this by the names she gave her sons. What did she say concerning each son?

   a. Reuben

   b. Simeon

   c. Levi

   d. Judah

5. (Personal) How many present-day "Leahs" know the Lord better and can fully trust Him even though they have been neglected by their husbands? The same can be true of a man who is neglected by his wife. If you have this situation in your life, are you able to put your full trust in the Lord and let Him carry your troubles?

6 a. **Challenge:** Describe in your own words what Psalm 37:5-8 advises the Christian who is in trouble.

b. Which Bible verse did you choose to hide in your heart this week by memorizing it?

GOD'S PRESENCE BRINGS PEACE, PROTECTION AND PROVISION

Genesis 28:10-22—29

Study Notes

Jacob's Dream at Bethel Genesis 28:10-22

We see in Genesis 28:10 that Jacob left home. All alone he traveled over rough country, up and down rocky hills, and across sandy deserts from Beer-sheba, Jacob's home, to Haran where his uncle Laban lived. We do not know how much baggage Jacob carried on his shoulder or on the back of an animal, but we know that he was carrying a heavy load in his heart.

Jacob was going to a land where he had never been before and was wondering if he would ever see home again. Alone in a strange land, he could easily imagine trouble behind every stone, as he thought of his offended brother lurking in the shadows. He was probably also remembering the last embrace of his doting mother!

To make the journey of over 400 miles from Beer-sheba to Haran would take days and would be like traveling from Los Angeles to San Francisco. The first day Jacob traveled about 43 miles from Beer-sheba going 12 miles south of Hebron to Bethel, a place about 11 miles north of where David established Jerusalem. That first day's trip was through a valley covered with large sheets of bare rock that looked almost like gravestones.

No hotels or motels lay along Jacob's way! He had no place to sleep except upon the ground. Perhaps Jacob, although he was a grown man, had never spent the night away from home before, and certainly not all alone in a desolate wilderness.

When the sun began going down, he looked about for a place to sleep. And there among the bleak hills were only the humps of gray rocks and thorny, rough shrubs. The ground was covered with loose stones of all sizes. He took a stone for a pillow and laid down on the hard ground to sleep.

How homesick Jacob must have been. No doubt he was sorry he had deceived his father and cheated his brother. He was not only homesick, but was probably afraid that Esau might have followed him or that some wild animal might attack him during the night. He must have looked up at the stars and thought about God. But God, too, seemed to be far away to Jacob. Exhausted from his hard journey, he finally fell asleep.

As he slept, Jacob was honored with a special communication from God. Jacob had a vision from heaven. In that day there was no written Word of God and therefore God spoke in personal messages such as in this dream.

"Long ago God spoke in many different ways to our fathers through the prophets [in visions, dreams, and even face-to-face], telling them little by little about his plans" (Hebrews 1:1). This is what happened to Jacob.

Today we are fortunate to have the recorded Word of God, the Bible, through which He can speak to us daily if we will take time to read it. Even when we do not have our Bible with us, the Holy Spirit can remind us of something about the Lord Jesus Christ (John 14:26).

Jacob had a vision of a ladder, a shining ladder of light, which reached down from heaven to earth (Genesis 28:12). Perhaps Jacob had been thinking about the distance between God and himself and his need to bridge that gap. In his dream, Jacob saw angels of God ascending and descending upon the ladder (Genesis 28:12).

We read much in the Bible about angels who are sent from God to minister to believers (Hebrews 1:14). In the Old Testament a promise is given, "Behold, I send an Angel before thee, to keep thee in the way, and to bring thee into the place which I have prepared" (Exodus 23:20).

Psalm 91:11,12 tells us, "For he shall give his angels charge over thee, to keep thee in all thy ways. They shall bear thee up in their hands lest thou dash thy foot against a stone." I do not believe that we will know fully until we stand before the Lord in heaven how His angels have ministered to us while we walked this earth as human beings.

Then a most wonderful thing happened—Jacob heard the divine voice of the Lord. Once again God renewed the promise He had made to Abraham and Isaac. He promised to give Jacob the very thing he had tried to obtain unfairly.

"And behold the Lord stood above it and said, 'I am the Lord, the God of Abraham your father [this means ancestor] and the God of Isaac: the land on which you lie I will give to you and to your descendants; and your descendants shall be like the dust of the earth, and you shall spread abroad to the west and to the east and to the north and to the south; and by you and your descendants shall all the families of the earth bless themselves" (Genesis 28:13,14).

The phrase in Genesis 28:14, "and by you and your descendants shall all the families of the earth bless themselves," is the promise that the birth of the Lord Jesus Christ will come through the line of Abraham's family. As Jacob was Abraham's grandson, so the Lord Jesus Christ would come through his line.

Yes, indeed, we have been blessed. The way has been made open to heaven through the Lord Jesus Christ's coming and giving Himself on the cross, taking upon Himself all our sins (Galatians 1:4, Ephesians 1:6,7).

We receive many blessings when we receive the Lord Jesus Christ as our Savior. Among them is God's peace, which is far more wonderful than the human mind can understand. His peace will keep your heart quiet and at rest as you trust in Christ Jesus (Philippians 4:7). We can also count upon the fact that God will supply all of our needs from His riches in glory because of what Christ Jesus has done for all of us (Philippians 4:19).

The Holy Spirit comes into our lives when we receive Jesus Christ by faith. We are marked as belonging to Christ by the Holy Spirit. "His presence within us is God's guarantee that he really will give us all that he promised; and the Spirit's seal upon us means that God has already purchased us and that he guarantees to bring us to himself. This is just one more reason for us to praise our glorious God" (Ephesians 1:14).

As we let the Holy Spirit control our lives, we receive other blessings from God. He produces within us His fruit of love, joy, peace, patience, kindness, goodness, faithfulness, gentleness, and self-control (Galatians 5:22,23).

God made a promise to Jacob in Genesis 28:15 which each Christian can claim for his own life. As you place your name in the blanks in this verse, you will realize what a comfort it was when God spoke these words to Jacob. What a comfort it can be to you today as you claim this promise for yourself.

"Behold, I am with _____ and will keep _____

127

wherever _____ go, and will bring you back to this land; for I will not leave _____ until I have done that of which I have spoken to _____."

Jacob was alone, frightened, and very weary after his long journey. Do you feel alone, frightened, and very weary? Claim this promise for yourself today.

When Jacob awoke from his sleep he said, "Surely the Lord is in this place, and I did not know it" (Genesis 28:16). He had been afraid and felt very lonely. We, too, may feel very lonely and afraid and yet we must realize that the Lord is in this place with us if we belong to Him.

His promises hold true for us today just as much as they did for Jacob long ago. Are we willing to say boldly, "The Lord is my helper, and I will not fear what man shall do unto me?" (Hebrews 13:6). *Our prayer should be "Lord, make us conscious of thy presence."*

In Genesis 28:17 we find Jacob saying, "How dreadful [or how awful] is this place." The Hebrew translation sets forth the idea that this is a feeling of reverence or awe and its root meaning actually is "to tremble." Jacob trembled in awe at having been in the presence of the Lord. Perhaps this was the first time in his life that he had been aware of the presence of God at his side.

This awareness of God's presence made him desire to worship God. We read in Genesis 28:18 that he rose up early in the morning and took a stone and set it up for an altar to God and there he worshiped God. The rocks were still there. The rough road still lay ahead. There was no person with him on his long journey. His home, his father, and mother, were all still behind him. His brother still hated him.

But how different now! Jacob no longer felt alone. He knew that the Lord was with him! He took the stone he had slept on as a pillow and used it to mark the very spot where God had appeared to him. Although out-of-doors, this place seemed like God's house and the very gate to heaven. So he called it Bethel, meaning "house of God." Although the dream was gone, the glory remained. *This was no passing fancy; this was reality that satisfied Jacob's soul.*

Today, because the Holy Spirit dwells in Christians (John 14:17), wherever we are is the "house of God!" Whether we are in our home, a car, a place of business, or walking down a street—God dwells there. Are you conscious that, if you are a Christian, the Holy Spirit lives within you no matter where you go or what your circumstances are?

Jacob was aware of God's presence and had a sound night's sleep after his vision. Do you have many fears for your safety, especially at night? Why not claim the parts of Genesis 28:15,16 which will assure

128

you that God is with you and will keep you just as He kept Jacob at night long ago?

"He giveth his beloved sleep" (Psalm 127:2). Whether you rest your head on a stone or a pillow, commit yourself to Him and rest in God's promise to care for you (Romans 5:8; 2 Corinthians 6:16; 1 Peter 3:12,13).

You may wonder why Jacob poured oil on the stone that he had set up as a pillar. We have no record that God commanded Jacob to do this, but in the law of Moses this act was a part of the service of consecration (Exodus 29:7; Leviticus 8:2,10,12,30; 1 Samuel 10:1). Oil, the symbol of the Holy Spirit, was poured on things and persons.

In Genesis 28:22 Jacob made a promise to the Lord that he would give Him a tenth of all that God had given to him. From the time of Moses to Jesus Christ, the tithe was a legal obligation of the Israelites (Leviticus 27:30). God gave a wonderful promise in Malachi 3:10 to those who would be faithful in giving their tithes to him: "Bring all the tithes into the storehouse so that there will be food enough in my Temple; if you do, I will open up the windows of heaven for you and pour out a blessing so great you won't have room enough to take it in! Try it! Let me prove it to you!"

Though the Christian has been freed from Old Testament law by the coming of the Lord Jesus Christ, tithing still brings great blessings. Everything belongs to God and with grateful hearts we are led to give back to Him a portion of what He has given so graciously to us (Matthew 6:1-4; 1 Corinthians 16:2; 2 Corinthians 9:6,7). God has also given the Christian the responsibility of helping others in need with the money He has given them (1 John 3:17-19).

An example of God's faithfulness and blessing after tithing one's income is the following true story. A young wife and mother attended a Bible class and discovered through her study that God loved her so much that He sent His only Son to forgive her sins (John 3:16,17). She received the Lord Jesus Christ in simple faith by inviting Him into her life (Revelation 3:20). She began to realize more and more how much God loved her and decided she wanted to express her love by giving a tithe.

Since her husband was not a Christian, she tithed from her household money. She said God never let them go hungry, and continued to meet every need of their household faithfully. She prayed that her husband would find her precious Savior.

Several years passed, and God continued to meet her needs beautifully. Then one day her husband found the joy that she had as he, too, received the Savior into his life. Today, God has led them into mission work abroad, and is continuing to pour out His blessings on them as they share His love with others in Africa.

Jacob Arrives in Haran and Meets Rachel Genesis 29:1-19

After Jacob saw the ladder and heard God's wonderful promise at Bethel, he continued on his way. When he reached a well in a field outside Haran, he found shepherds watching their flocks (Genesis 29:2). He saw Rachel, a beautiful young woman, coming to the well with her father's flock. Jacob rolled back a great stone from off the well and helped Rachel to water her sheep. He told her who he was and she ran and told her father, Laban. Laban came and welcomed Jacob into his home (Genesis 29:4-14).

"For the Lord's portion is his people, Jacob his allotted heritage. *He found him* in a desert land, and in the howling waste of the wilderness; *he encircled him, he cared for him, he kept him* as the apple of his eye. Like an eagle that stirs up its nest, that flutters over its young, spreading out its wings, catching them, bearing them on its pinions, *the Lord alone did lead him,* and there was no foreign God with him" (Deuteronomy 32:9-12).

In a sense this passage could be referring to the nation of Israel. However, as we think of Jacob it could apply very much to him as part of the nation of Israel. God carried him safely to Haran through the desert land. He led him to the well and instructed him to water the sheep.

As Moses recorded what God did for Jacob, do you realize that He wants to do the same thing for you, a Christian, today? Underline in the notes the portion which you would like to claim for yourself this week.

We read in Genesis 29:2,3 that there was a very large stone over the well that watered the sheep. It had to be rolled back in order that the sheep could be watered. Think of the well as symbolic of the Word of God, the Bible.

Some people do not go to the Bible themselves. They are like sheep sitting around the well! They wait for the preachers and teachers to roll back the stone over the well and to give them the water of the Word of God, the Bible. Yet, we are instructed in the Scriptures that if we are to know God's blessings and promises, we need to "water" our own lives by reading the Bible daily.

"The whole Bible was given to us by inspiration from God and is useful to teach us what is true and to make us realize what is wrong in our lives; it straightens us out and helps us do what is right. It is God's way of making us well prepared at every point, fully equipped to do good to everyone" (2 Timothy 3:16,17). "Study to shew thyself approved unto God, a workman that needeth not to be ashamed, rightly dividing the word of truth" (2 Timothy 2:15). Also read John 20:31, and Romans 15:4.

Do you "thirst" and want to personally drink from the Bible daily by reading it? Are you willing to pray and ask God to give you this desire in your heart right now?

A study of women in the Bible is revealing. In a previous lesson we read that Rebekah, Jacob's mother, was a hard worker, and yet she was full of joy and at peace in her work. Remember that she drew water for all of the camels of Eliezer, the servant, who was sent to obtain a wife for Isaac? (Genesis 24:18,19)

Now we see that her niece, Laban's daughter Rachel, was the same type of woman. We find her watching and caring for the sheep. What a difference it makes in the home when women understand that it is most pleasing to the Lord when they are faithful homemakers.

Remember that God does have a plan for your life. He wants you to seek out His plan each day as you read the Bible and pray. As you give yourself to the work He has for you, you'll find the Lord constantly with you, providing encouragement and power for you to do your task enthusiastically and successfully.

Proverbs 31:10-31 gives us a pattern for a good Christian woman's life. Many thoughts in these verses will impress you as to what a good Christian woman should be like. "A good wife who can find? She is far more precious than jewels. The heart of her husband trusts in her, and he will have no lack of gain" (Proverbs 31:10,11).

"Strength and dignity are her clothing, and she laughs at the time to come. She opens her mouth with wisdom, and the teaching of kindness is on her tongue" (Proverbs 31:25,26).

"Charm is deceitful, and beauty is vain, but a woman who fears the Lord is to be praised. Give her of the fruit of her hands, and let her works praise her in the gates" (Proverbs 31:30,31).

This passage in Proverbs does not mean God's plan is that every woman marry. But it gives us a pattern for a gracious Christian wife who is blessed by the Lord. The modern trend is to complain that Christians don't want their wives to work outside of the home. But we must realize that God has a different plan for each Christian woman. Some are to remain in the home and not to work. For others it is necessary economically for them to do some work outside the home.

Note that in Proverbs 31:24 this woman makes linen garments and sells them; undoubtedly she was able to make them in her home and care for her children at the same time. This plan is the wisest for

131

a Christian mother. She should pray that the Lord will lead her into some type of work that can be done at her home if she needs to add to the family income, particularly when children arein the home.

WOMEN'S LIBERATION

Lord, it seems like
    the devil is doing a nice business
        with a respectable cause
            Women's Liberation!

They tell me that I am not
    a household drudge
    a sex object
    intellectually inferior
    simpler and weaker
You told me that a long time ago, Lord
When you said in Genesis, chapter 2
    that woman was a help-mate to man.

I've been told I should be liberated from this
    sad condition
        I am to have
            equal pay
                equal opportunity
                    sexual freedom
                    and a job.

Well, I have a job, Lord
    I am the help-mate to my husband
        a homemaker
        a mother
The pay is fair, and I don't feel deprived of
    opportunity.

My life is
    alive
        interesting
            fun
                challenging
                    surprising
                    and fulfilling
Thank you, God, for making me, a woman.

—Doris Greig

Whether you are a man or a woman reading these notes, will you remember that God does have a plan for your life? He wants you to seek out His plan each day as you read the Bible and pray. As you give yourself to the work He has for you, you'll find the Lord constantly with you, providing encouragement and power for you to do your task enthusiastically and successfully.

"He gives power to the tired and worn out, and strength to the weak" (Isaiah 40:29). "For I can do everything God asks me to with the help of Christ who gives me the strength and power" (Philippians 4:13).

Only one life,
'twill soon be past.
Only what's done for Christ will last.

—C. T. Studd

Laban Tricks Jacob; The Birth of Leah's Sons Genesis 29:20-35

Jacob went to work for Laban and was very happy in that household. Jacob loved Rachel dearly and wanted her to be his wife. He made an agreement with her father to work for seven years before he could marry her. But at the end of seven years, instead of giving him Rachel, the girl he loved, Laban cheated Jacob and tricked him into marrying her older sister, Leah.

Right here we see Jacob having to reap what he had sown. He had cheated his brother, deceived his father, and now he was being paid back. The one who tricked others was now tricked by Laban (Galatians 6:7).

The excuse that Laban offered is found in Genesis 29:25 and 26. That the younger daughter be married before the first-born daughter was not customary. In Genesis 29:30 we find that because Jacob loved Rachel, he agreed to serve seven more years for her. Laban then gave Rachel to Jacob in marriage. The custom in that country was for a man to have more than one wife. But this was not God's original plan, for he created only one wife for Adam.

In Genesis 29:17 we read that Leah was tender-eyed but Rachel was beautiful and well favored. "Tender-eyed" may mean that she had something wrong with her eyes, although no one is sure what the problem was. In Genesis 29:30 we read that Jacob loved Rachel more than Leah. But the Lord saw Leah's predicament and noticed that she was neglected by her husband, Jacob.

It is an amazing fact that nothing escapes the notice of the Lord.

133

True, Rachel was the wife whom Jacob had chosen, and that he was tricked into marrying Leah first. Yet the Lord was watching all of this and He worked it out for the greatest good of all concerned. The children born to Leah and Rachel and their maids were the founders of the 12 tribes of Israel. Yes, Leah seemed to be the ugly duckling, but the Lord heard her cry.

We gain real spiritual insight into Leah's life by the names she gave her sons (Genesis 29:31). The first son was named Reuben which means "surely the Lord hath looked upon my affliction; now therefore my husband will love me" (Genesis 29:32). The second son was named Simeon, "because the Lord hath heard that I was hated, he hath therefore given me this son also" (Genesis 29:33). The third son was named Levi, "now this time will my husband be joined unto me, because I have born him three sons" (Genesis 29:34).

The fourth son was named Judah, "now will I praise the Lord" (Genesis 29:35). *With this last name she seemed to recognize that she would never receive the love from a man that she could receive from her Lord.* And thus she said, "Now I will praise the Lord."

How many women are there today who are like Leah? How many women know the Lord better because they have been neglected by their husbands? A woman always desires to hold the attention of the man she married. And when she fails, possibly because of a fault in the man rather than in herself, the blow to her pride can lead her to a full and complete trust in the Lord.

The same can be true for a man who has been cast aside by a woman. If you are in such circumstances or have been through such a trial, will you say as Leah did, "Now I will praise the Lord?" Doing so will release your problem to the Lord and you will learn to trust Him more fully through this prayer. *Let the Lord carry your troubles as you praise Him.*

Many verses in the Bible tell us the Lord is our deliverer in trouble. "The Lord is my rock, and my fortress, and my deliverer; my God, my strength in whom I will trust; my buckler, and the horn of my salvation, and my high tower" (Psalm 18:2). Psalm 37:5-8 teaches us to commit and trust the Lord and He will act for us. He will show forth His goodness.

Will you rest and wait patiently on the Lord as this psalm says? Don't fret about other people's sinful actions and how they succeed. Don't be angry and don't do any evil!

Lamentations 3:25 tells us "The Lord is good unto them that wait for him, to the soul that seeketh him." Nahum 1:7 adds to this thought, "The Lord is good, a strong hold in the day of trouble."

Will you trust Him in your day of trouble? Perhaps yoursisn't even Leah's type of situation. Yet if you have any trouble in your life, you can apply these promises to the Lord and trust in Him. Will you do this this week?

"See that no one pays back evil for evil, but always try to do good to each other and to everyone else. Always be joyful. Always keep on praying. No matter what happens, always be thankful, for this is God's will for you who belong to Christ Jesus. Do not smother the Holy Spirit" (1 Thessalonians 5:15-19).

Study Questions

Before you begin your study this week:
1. Pray and ask God to speak to you through His Holy Spirit each day.
2. Use only your Bible for your answers.
3. Write your answers and the verses you have used.
4. Challenge questions are for those who have the time and wish to do them.
5. Personal questions are to be shared with your study group only if you wish to share.
6. As you study look for a verse to memorize this week. Write it down, carry it with you, tack it to your bulletin board, tape it to the dashboard of your car. Make a real effort to learn the verse and its reference.

FIRST DAY: Read all of the preceding notes and look up all the Scriptures.

1. What was a helpful or new thought from the overview of Genesis 28:10-22 and 29?

2. What personal application did you select to apply to your own life?

SECOND DAY: Read all of Genesis 30, concentrating on verses 1-24.

1 a. What emotions did Rachel display when she could have no children, and whom did she blame?

   b. What was Jacob's reaction to Rachel's emotions?

   c. Who did Jacob say had withheld children from Rachel?

2 a. Apparently Rachel nagged Jacob about not having children. What do you believe she should have done about her childless-

ness? See Genesis 25:21; 1 Samuel 1:9-11; and James 4:15.

b. (Personal) The "impossible" situations in our lives can include loneliness, misunderstanding, emotional problems, and financial difficulties. Do you have a problem? Are you willing to pray to God the prayer that Jesus Christ prayed in Matthew 26:39?

3. **Challenge:** Jacob became angry with Rachel. The Bible speaks of husband-wife relationships in the following verses. Try to put these thoughts into your own words.

Ephesians 5:22,23

Ephesians 5:25,26

4. Read Romans 8:28,29 and 2 Chronicles 20:15 in *The Living Bible,* if possible, and record their encouraging message.

5 a. The custom was that a woman give her maid to her husband and claim the child born by this union as her own. Certainly this was not God's plan for His people, the Israelites. How many children did Rachel's maid-servant give to Jacob? How many children did Leah's maidservant give to Jacob?

b. What was the name of the daughter born to Jacob by Leah?

6 a. At last, Rachel bore a son. What did she name him and what did she say after his birth?

137

b. Look back through Genesis 29:31-34, Genesis 30:4-22, and Genesis 35:22-26 and list all 12 sons of Jacob. These names and men are important for from them were formed the 12 tribes of Israel.

THIRD DAY: Read Genesis 30:25-43.

1 a. What did Jacob ask Laban to do after his son Joseph was born?

b. What did Laban say the Lord had done for him because Jacob had served him?

c. What did he offer Jacob if he would stay?

2. From Genesis 30:29,30 what was the evidence that the Lord had blessed Laban because Jacob had been a faithful servant?

3 a. **Challenge:** Jacob was a good servant to Laban. As Christians we are to be good employees also. What does Colossians 3:22-24 say concerning this?

b. (Personal) What kind of an employee are you? Do you need to ask God today to change your attitude and actions, whether you work at home or outside of your home?

4 a. What did Jacob ask Laban for in Genesis 30:31-33?

b. What did Laban do to treat Jacob dishonestly concerning his request in Genesis 30:31? Give verses.

5 a. The Bible has guidelines for the employer. Laban mistreated Jacob, his employee of 14 years. What does Leviticus 25:43 say concerning the employer?

b. (Personal) What kind of an employer are you? Do you need to ask the Lord to change some of your attitudes and actions right now?

6 a. Jacob became rich in material things (Genesis 30:43). What does Ephesians 1:7 and Ephesians 2:4,5 tell you about God's spiritual riches and how we may receive them?

b. (Personal) Have you received God's spiritual riches by receiving His Son, the Lord Jesus Christ? (Ephesians 2:8,9; Hebrews 12:2)

FOURTH DAY: Read Genesis 31, concentrating on verses 1-21.

1 How did Laban and his sons feel toward Jacob after he had become a wealthy man as described in Genesis 30:43?

2 a. What did the Lord tell Jacob to do?

b. What did God say to Jacob in Genesis 31:3? He had already promised Jacob this in Genesis 28:15.

c. Was Jacob conscious that God had been with him during his 20 years in Haran with Laban's family? Give verse from Genesis 31.

d. To whom did Jacob give the credit for giving him all his cattle? Give verse.

139

3. **Challenge:** Just as God gave cattle to Jacob (Genesis 30:30), God provides for us as Christians according to our needs—whether they be physical or spiritual. How do the following verses help you to understand God's care for you? Put them into your own words.

   Philippians 2:13 and 1 Thessalonians 5:24

   Philippians 4:19

4 a. In Matthew 6:33 we are instructed to seek the kingdom of God and *His righteousness. What does Isaiah 64:6 say about human righteousness? Note*: Righteousness means to have a way of life which is just, upright, virtuous and blameless according to God's standards.

   b. (Personal) Do you have your own righteousness, or do you have God's righteousness because you have received it by your faith in His Son, the Lord Jesus Christ? See Romans 10:9-11.

5 a. Did Rachel and Leah seem willing to go back to the land of Canaan with Jacob? See Genesis 31. Give verses for your answer.

   b. What did Rachel do before they left?

6. What were the circumstances of Jacob's departure according to Genesis 31:20,21?

FIFTH DAY: Read Genesis 31:22-42.

1 a. How long was it before Laban found out that Jacob had left, and how long did it take Laban to get to the hill country of Gilead which was near Jacob and his caravan?

   b. What did Laban tell Jacob in Genesis 31:27,28?

2. What was Jacob's reply to Laban about his "running away" from him to go to the land of Canaan?

3 a. Laban asked Jacob why he had stolen his household gods. What was Jacob's reply in Genesis 31:32?

   b. Laban searched all of the tents. Did he find the household gods?

   c. Where were the household gods and how were they concealed from Laban? Give verses.

4 a. How long had Jacob served Laban?

   b. What part of this time did he serve Laban for his block of cattle?

5. How does Rachel's lie about the household gods in Genesis 31:35 illustrate Romans 3:23?

6 a. What hope do you find in Romans 6:23?

   b (Personal) Do you have this hope in your life because of your faith in the Lord Jesus Christ as your Savior and Lord?

SIXTH DAY: Read Genesis 31:43-55.

1. What did Laban suggest that he and Jacob do in Genesis 31:44?

2. Look up the word "covenant" in the dictionary. What does it mean?

3. What was Jacob's reply to Laban in Genesis 31:45,46?

4. Who was to be the witness between Laban and Jacob to watch to see that Jacob did not "ill treat" his daughter? Give verse.

5. What did Jacob do in Genesis 31:54?

6 a. What did Laban do the next morning?

   b. Which verse from this lesson did you choose to memorize and claim for your life this week?

GOD ALWAYS REMEMBERS HIS OWN IN TIMES OF TROUBLE

Genesis 30-31

Study Notes

Introduction

In these two chapters we find a record of the increase of Jacob's family. In Genesis 29 Leah bore Jacob four sons—Reuben, Simon, Levi and Judah (verses 32-35). Two more sons were born by Bilhah, Rachel's maid. These sons' names are Dan and Naphtali (Genesis 30:6-8).

Next we find that Jacob had two more sons by Zilpah, Leah's maid (Genesis 30:9-13). These two sons of Jacob were named Gad and Asher. Leah again bore Jacob two sons (Genesis 30:17-20), Issachar and Zebulun.

And then Joseph was born to Jacob by Rachel in Genesis 30:22-24. We find recorded later in Genesis 35:16-18 that Rachel again bore one last son to Jacob who was named Benjamin. *All of these sons are very important, for from them were formed the 12 tribes of Israel.* Count the names of these sons in this paragraph and you will confirm they are 12.

Later in our reading in the Old Testament we will discover that Joseph's two sons, Ephraim and Manasseh, formed two of the tribes, while no tribal territory was allotted to Levi, for they became the priestly line (Genesis 48:5; Numbers 26:5-51; Joshua 13:7-33,15-19).

Before the Israelites entered the promised land, two of the tribes Reuben and Gad, and half of Manasseh chose to settle on the east side of the Jordan (Numbers 32:33).

During the time of the rule of the judges of Israel, each tribe was a law unto itself. When David became king over the whole land the 12 tribes were unified. David then appointed a captain over each tribe (1 Chronicles 27:16-22). The captivities of the Jewish people later wiped out these tribal distinctions.

Rachel Is Jealous of Jacob's Other Children Until She Bears Joseph Genesis 30:1-24

Rachel was envious of Leah who had given Jacob four sons. Rachel was barren and blamed Jacob for her childless state as she said, "Give me children, or else I die" (Genesis 30:1). Perhaps she was proud of her beauty and the fact that Jacob had served 14 years for her and desired her more than her sister, Leah. This pride undoubtedly caused her to also want to be first in giving children to Jacob. We find that Jacob's anger was kindled because Rachel nagged him about her barrenness.

Jacob spoke the truth when he said, "Am I in God's stead, who hath withheld from thee the fruit of the womb?" (Genesis 30:2) Jacob was trying to point out to Rachel that children were a gift from the Lord. "Lo, children are an heritage of the Lord: and the fruit of the womb is his reward" (Psalm 127:3).

Rachel was wrong to nag Jacob and to blame him that she had borne no children. When a woman nags her husband, she acts contrary to the will of God, for God never nags.

What could Rachel and Jacob have done in these circumstances? In Scripture are helpful examples of how others handled such situations:

Isaac, the husband of Rebekah, prayed for his wife to have a child (Genesis 25:21).

Hannah wept and prayed for a child. She promised the Lord that if He would give her a son she would give him back to the Lord all the days of his life (see 1 Samuel 1:9-11).

James 4:15 declares, "If the Lord will, we shall live, and do this, or that." Rachel was unwilling to submit herself to the will of the Lord. Her attitude is a warning to us. Our prayers should be, "Lord, deliver us from nagging others and make us submissive to your will for our lives."

Childlessness was the "impossible" situation that made Rachel so unhappy. Many such situations in life face every person. What is your seemingly impossible situation?

144

Is it loneliness, misunderstanding, emotional problems, financial difficulties, family problems, spiritual insecurity or something else? *Whatever your problem is, if you will turn to the Lord Jesus Christ and trust Him with your problem, He will not fail you.* Pray the prayer that the Lord Jesus Christ prayed in Matthew 26:39: "Nevertheless not as I will, but as thou wilt." Then trust God to uphold and help you in your difficulty according to His perfect plan for your life.

The Bible speaks about a wife's attitudes toward her husband and the husband's attitude toward his wife. These principles can also apply in business and friend relationships. Proverbs 25:24 tells us, "It is better to live in a corner of the housetop than in a house shared with a contentious woman." Proverbs 25:28, "A man without self-control is like a city broken into and left without walls."

If you are a Christian and have some trouble in your life right now, claim Romans 5:5 for yourself. "The love of God is shed abroad in our hearts by the Holy Ghost which is given unto us." Count on the love of God to see you through whatever trouble there is. Listen for God's voice to you today in your time of trouble.

A lawful custom of the pagan countries was that a woman could give her maid to her husband and claim the children born of this union as her own. Certainly this was not God's plan for His people, the Israelites. Yet Rachel, acting out of the will of God, gave her maid Bilhah to Jacob as a wife. In Genesis 30:5 Bilhah conceived. And in Genesis 30:7 again Bilhah conceived and bore Jacob a second son.

Leah also followed this pagan practice and in Genesis 30:9 gave Zilpah, her maid, to Jacob to wife and she, too, bore Jacob two sons. Thus we see both Rachel and Leah used worldly ways to procure children for their husband, Jacob.

We, too, are guilty of trying to plan and accomplish things in our lives by the world's ways rather than waiting on God to act in our lives according to His perfect plan. In the long run it is only God's ways which will satisfy our lives.

"Let them thank the Lord for his steadfast love, for his wonderful works to the sons of men! For he satisfies him who is thirsty, and the hungry he fills with good things" (Psalm 107:8,9). "And my people shall be satisfied with my goodness, says the Lord" (Jeremiah 31:14).

The world may try to make you think it can bless you as a Christian, but remember, "Every good gift and every perfect gift is from above, and cometh down from the Father of lights" (James 1:17). We should never expect anything of lasting value and constant joy except from our Heavenly Father.

The world seldom keeps its promises, but our Lord never changes (Malachi 3:6; Hebrews 6:17,18). On this fact rests our faith and the continual supply of our needs. Will you pray, "Lord, teach me to rest

145

in faith and trust you in my daily experiences."

Note that Dinah, the name of the daughter Leah bore Jacob, is recorded in Genesis 30:21. Also note Genesis 30:14-17, a passage you may have found difficult to understand. Leah's son, Reuben, in the days of the wheat harvest, went to the field, found mandrakes and brought them to his mother.

Rachel asked Leah for the mandrakes because of superstitious belief that a love potion could be made from them. What the mandrakes were is uncertain, as critics are not agreed about them. The reference here could be to fruits, flowers or roots.

Some think the mandrakes were jasmine flowers which have a pleasant scent. Others believe them to be "love apples," a yellow, plumlike fruit that grew on a tuberous root and when eaten was supposed to act as a love potion. This particular fruit ripens in May, the same time of the year as the wheat harvest mentioned in Genesis 30:14. Still other theologians believe the mandrakes in Genesis 30 refer to a forked root that in shape resembles a man.

The fact that the Bible states Leah and Rachel believed a mandrake could be made into a love potion does not mean their belief is correct. When the Bible mentions such a false belief as this one, Scripture is simply recording what a particular people believed. God's Word is *not* teaching that this belief is either true or correct.

Is it not true that many people still follow superstitions today? Are you guilty of this? With God's help we can refrain from following the superstitions of this world.

In Genesis 30:22 we see that God did remember Rachel and opened her womb. She bore a son to Jacob and named him Joseph. In a day when bearing sons was the most important thing in life for any woman, Rachel had been in deepest misery because of her barrenness. In His own time the Lord answered her great desire and gave her this son from her own body. In Genesis 30:23 Rachel said, "God hath taken away my reproach."

Jacob Asks Laban to Let Him Return Home to Canaan Genesis 30:25-43

After Rachel had born Joseph, Jacob went to his father-in-law and asked him for permission to go to his own home and country with his wives and children. Laban claimed to have received special knowledge by magic or divination from his household gods that he must keep Jacob around to guarantee his prosperity. Remember that Laban was not a follower of God. His household gods were idols made by human hands which he worshiped.

In Genesis 30:28 Laban told Jacob that he could name his wages if he would stay. Yes, Jacob had been a faithful servant and Laban had been blessed by Jacob's faithfulness! He had few cattle when Jacob came, and now with Jacob's management he had a multitude (Genesis 30:29,30).

Jacob was a good servant to Laban. As Christians we are to be good employees also. *The Bible teaches us that we are to serve well in all areas and we are to do everything enthusiastically, for we are not only serving our employer but we are also serving God.*

We are taught that even if we don't like our employer, we are to work heartily as unto the Lord! We are also told to be obedient to our employer and to please him by working well and faithfully (Colossians 3:22-24, Titus 2:9).

Are you in a situation where you feel you have an employer or someone above you who is not treating you fairly? The Bible has instructions for the Christian in this circumstance also. "Don't repay evil for evil . . . . Instead, pray for God's help for them, for we are to be kind to others, and God will bless us" (1 Peter 3:9). Will you ask the Lord to give you His kindness?

Jacob asked Laban for part of the herd in Genesis 30:31-33. He asked for every speckled and spotted goat and every black lamb. Now in that day there were very few speckled, spotted goats; most of them were plain white and most of the lambs were also white. Therefore, Jacob was not asking for too much.

Yet Laban treated Jacob dishonestly concerning his request and removed all the speckled and spotted goats and black sheep and sent them away with his sons. Laban himself stayed three days journey away from Jacob! (Genesis 30:35,36)

But Jacob was not to be discounted so easily. He decided to outwit his uncle. In Genesis 30:37-42 we read of the methods by which he tried to do this. First of all he subjected the ewes to prenatal influence (Genesis 30:37,38). Next he separated the newly born flock in such an arrangement that they would tend to bear spotted young (Genesis 30:40). And lastly he planned a way so that he could have the strongest of the newborn in the flock (Genesis 30:42).

Jacob believed that all his planning was the means by which he obtained many lambs and goats. Yet in the final analysis it was God who blessed Jacob with this herd. Often we plan and work to accomplish something and yet it is by God's own good pleasure that He blesses us.

The truth that God Himself provided Jacob with all of these flocks is revealed in the dream. "Then the angel of God said to me in a dream, 'Jacob, lift up your eyes and see, all the goats that leap upon the flock are striped, spotted, and mottled; for I have seen all that Laban is doing to you. I am the God of Bethel, where you anointed a

147

pillar and made a vow to me. Now arise, go forth from this land, and return to the land of your birth'" (Genesis 31:11-13).

As we look at Genesis 30:37-43 we see Jacob's reliance on his own wiles and strategies to enlarge his wealth before he leaves Laban. He did not recognize that God would bless him if he just simply waited upon Him for these things. Actually the livestock he had which were of solid color had the hereditary factors for color in their genes, and the colored goats and lambs could have been born by God's own providence without Jacob's plan.

We will see in Genesis 32 that before God allows Jacob to enter into the Promised Land, He will bring about a circumstance that will break Jacob's confidence in himself and his own abilities and strategies. *God will teach Jacob to rely completely upon His power and blessing alone.*

Jacob Flees from Laban Genesis 31:1-21

Laban's sons felt that Jacob had taken all their father's riches, and Laban himself did not regard Jacob with favor as he had before. In Genesis 31:3 the Lord told Jacob to return to the land of his father and to his relatives and again promised, "I will be with you." This same promise was given to Jacob in Genesis 28:15 when God said, "Behold, I am with you and will keep you wherever you go, and will bring you back to this land; for I will not leave you until I have done that of which I have spoken to you."

Notice in Genesis 28:15 that God also promised to bring Jacob back to his own land, and now we find in Genesis 31:3 that God told him to return to the land of his fathers. Rachel and Leah were called to Jacob and he told them of his desire to return as God had called him back to his homeland. Jacob mentioned to them that their father, whom he had served with all his strength, had cheated him and changed his wages 10 times.

Some employers today also are unfair to their employees. The Bible has clear teachings about such relationships. The Scriptures tell us that we are not to rule with rigor over anyone, but we are to fear the Lord (Leviticus 25:43). Many places tell us that the laborer is worthy of his hire (1 Timothy 5:18). In Colossians 4:1 the employer is cautioned to be just and equal to each employee, knowing that the Master in heaven is just and equal with him.

What kind of an employer are you? *Do you need to ask the Lord to change some of your attitudes and actions toward your employees?*

Jacob went on to tell Rachel and Leah of the dream which God sent to him in Genesis 31:10-13. Rachel and Leah agreed to return

148

with Jacob to Canaan. They felt that their father had sold them and now regarded them as foreigners.

Their closing statement in Genesis 31:16 should be the heart attitude of every good woman toward her husband, "Whatever God has said to you, do." Is this your life attitude in your family toward your husband, your children, your friends and your associates?

Jacob arose without telling Laban that he intended to flee. He quickly put his sons and wives on camels and drove away all of his cattle that he had gained. He left Laban's land and headed toward his homeland of Canaan where his father, Isaac, lived.

While Jacob was busy doing all of this, Laban was out shearing his sheep. Rachel stole her father's household gods (Genesis 31:19). She did not tell Jacob that she had done this. These household gods gave the privilege of leadership in a family. Nuzu tablets from the 15th century B.C. indicate that possession of the household gods marked a man as the chief heir.

Apparently Rachel did not trust in God to provide for her needs. She wanted to make sure that Jacob would have the legal claim to all of Laban's estate rather than his own sons who were mentioned in Genesis 31:1. This was a very wrong thing for Rachel to do and showed her lack of dependence upon God at this point in her life.

"So don't be anxious about tomorrow. God will take care of your tomorrow too. Live one day at a time" (Matthew 6:34). Are you willing to trust God with your today and tomorrow?

Laban Finds Jacob Genesis 31:22-42

In Genesis 31:21 Jacob crossed the Euphrates and "set his face toward the hill country of Gilead." *This passage contains a lesson on how to learn the will of the Lord in making daily decisions:*

First, Jacob expressed the natural *human* desire to return home in Genesis 30:25, "Send me away, that I may go to my own home and country."

Second, circumstances combined to make it impossible for him to remain with Laban (Genesis 31:1,2). Laban's sons did not approve of him and Laban himself did not.

Third, the Lord gave him a formal command to leave in Genesis 31:3.

These three factors are always present when a believer is truly yielded to the plan of the Lord: *The Lord's will is revealed to us through His written Word today, through circumstances, and through the desire of our hearts if we are truly yielded to the will of God.* If the Lord's command has not been given, we must recognize that the time is not yet right.

Meekness is yieldedness. We must be meek. "The meek will he guide in judgment: and the meek will he teach his way" (Psalm 25:9). Let our prayer be today, "Lord, lead me."

The third day after Jacob had fled, Laban was informed. Laban took his relatives with him and for seven days followed Jacob into the hill country of Gilead. God came to Laban in a dream and told him to deal gently with Jacob (Genesis 31:24).

Our big words have little meaning when they are not backed up by small gestures. The daily words of love, the daily acts of unselfishness or deeds of kindness speak much louder than the declared affection rendered only on a special occasion. We should all pray, "Lord, make us more thoughtful of our loved ones."

Laban confronted Jacob and asked him why he cheated him by secretly running away with his daughters rather than allowing him to give him a farewell party. Jacob's reply to Laban indicated that he was afraid that Laban would keep his daughters by force (Genesis 31:31). Considering Laban's treatment of Jacob during the past 20 years, one can understand how Jacob might have feared that Laban would have tried to cheat him.

After all, he had cheated Jacob by giving him Leah for his wife when he had served for Rachel. He had cheated him concerning the flocks by removing all the speckled and black sheep and lambs from his flocks before putting Jacob in charge of them (Genesis 30:35). Laban complained that Jacob had stolen his daughters, yet Jacob had served seven years for each daughter, just as Laban had ordered. In reality, Laban had cheated Jacob and given him just cause to fear him.

Laban's attitude reminds us of those who give flowers to mother on Mother's Day and then forget her the rest of the year. Of course, we let her do dishes and baby-sit for the grandchildren, yet without our showing her any gratitude.

Our big words have little meaning when they are not backed up by small gestures. The daily words of love, the daily acts of unselfishness or deeds of kindness speak much louder than the declared affection rendered only on a special occasion. We should all pray, "Lord, make us more thoughtful of our loved ones."

Laban asked Jacob, "But why did you steal my gods?" (Genesis 31:30)

Jacob did not realize that Rachel had stolen the gods and so he stated, "Any one with whom you find your gods shall not live" (Genesis 31:32).

Laban went into Jacob's tent, Leah's tent, into the tent of the two maid servants and finally into Rachel's tent. He searched for the household gods and found them nowhere. Where were they hidden?

We read in Genesis 31:34 that Rachel had put them in the camel's saddle and sat upon them. When her father entered the tent she told him that she was sorry that she could not get up. Therefore, Laban searched her tent but did not find the household gods.

Laban's own daughter had been a very good pupil in his school of cunning and now outwitted her father. This should be a lesson to all parents. Ask the Lord to help you set a good example before your children so that they will learn the right lessons.

Rachel's lie about the household gods illustrates what the Bible says in Romans 3:23, "All have sinned, and come short of the glory of God"—including Rachel! Yes, *all* have sinned, including ourselves. We find great hope as we read in Romans 6:23, "The wages of sin is death; but the gift of God is eternal life through Jesus Christ our Lord."

Have you this hope in your life because of your faith in Jesus Christ as your Savior and Lord?

Jacob and Laban Covenant Genesis 31:43-55

Laban suggested to Jacob that they make a covenant and let it be a witness between them (Genesis 31:44). The Hebrew says, "Let us cut a covenant." It was a blood covenant, clear recognition by Laban of Jacob's claims and signifying the end of the feud between them.

The heap of stones was set up as a memorial to the covenant (Genesis 31:46). Laban and Jacob ate there beside the memorial, as a sign of their restored fellowship and peace with one another (Genesis 31:46). The heap formed what was called Mizpah or "outlook point." This was where a person could see the entire country in both directions.

The word *Mizpah* itself indicated suspicion and lack of trust. By raising such a heap, Jacob and Laban signified that they were inviting God to sit in the look-out post to keep watch over two people who could not be trusted. God was thus invited to watch over both Jacob and Laban so strife could be avoided.

"This heap is a witness, and the pillar is a witness, that I will not pass over this heap to you, and you will not pass over this heap and this pillar to me, for harm" (Genesis 31:52). Jacob was promising to care for Laban's daughters with kindness and consideration. Both

Laban and Jacob were promising that they would not pass this point on the border to do violence to one another.

Here both parties of the covenant spent the night and ate together (Genesis 31:54), and then early in the morning Laban arose and kissed his grandchildren and his daughters and blessed them. He departed and returned home to Padan-aram. Jacob went on to the land of Canaan.

AFTERWORD

In our first study of Genesis, chapters 1-17, we focused on discovering God's power, as it was demonstrated again and again in the Creation—the creation of the universe, the creation of life in its many forms and, ultimately, in the creation of man in God's own image. We saw God's power again demonstrated at the time of the Flood, as He judged sin on the earth while saving Noah and his family. In the life of Abraham, we saw God's power further manifested on behalf of His friend and his descendants.

In this study of Genesis 18-31, we have been discovering here—even as we did in the previous study—that the God of power is also the God of promise. To that end, we have been seeking out and claiming God's promises for ourselves, as they have unfolded before us in the lives of Abraham, Isaac and Jacob.

In the final study of Genesis 32-50, we will discover together that this God of power and promise is also a God who protects His own. As the story of Jacob and his 12 sons continues, particularly in the life of Joseph, we see how God remains ever faithful to His often faithless children. He exercises His power to protect and preserve His chosen people through endless dangers and difficulties, even when such adversities are the result of their own failures, weaknesses and sins.

Why?

Because God's people are the People of the Promise—the promise that one day through them would come their Messiah. His coming would bless them and, through them, also bless all other nations on earth. He did come and live briefly among us (John 1:14), died for our sins (Romans 5:6,8), and rose again to take his place at the right hand of the Father where He now intercedes for us (Romans 8:34). He is, of course, Jesus Christ, God's only begotten Son (John 3:16), whom

153

through faith (Romans 3:22), we know and love (1 John 4:19) as our Lord and Savior Jesus Christ.

Do join us soon in our concluding and exciting study of Genesis 32-50, *Discovering God's Protection.*

Also Available in the Joy of Living Series. . . .

Courage to Conquer: Studies in Daniel—
by Doris W. Greig
A Joy of Living Bible Study in Daniel. This is an in-depth look at a companion of kings, leader of men and a man truly devoted to his God. Today's world can learn from his uncompromising example. A 6-week study. **5419489**

Walking in God's Way: Studies in Ruth and Esther—
by Ruth M. Bathauer and Doris W. Greig
A 7-week Joy of Living Bible Study. Learn about God's special love for us and how He is leading our every step. Explore how circumstances never stand in the way of God's perfect plan for our lives. **5419474**

Power for Positive Living: Studies in Philippians and Colossians—by Doris W. Greig
This Joy of Living Bible Study focuses on the Christian life of joy and hope as expressed in Philippians and Colossians. We can be joyful, even in a world of sorrow, and resist the powers of evil if we stand fast in the knowledge of our Lord. **5419493**

Exercising a Balanced Faith: Studies in James—by Doris W. Greig
Granted that we are saved "by grace through faith"—what is the role of good works? This 8-lesson course explains James' insistence that works demonstrate whether or not we have saving faith. **5419649**

Living in the Light: Studies in 1, 2 and 3 John—by Doris W. Greig
Recent scientific studies have shown the healthy effects of plenty of light. This 6-lesson study explores what it means spiritually to live an enlightened life—walking in the light of God's Word. **5419501**

Discovering God's Power: Studies in Genesis 1-17—by Doris W. Greig
"In the beginning was the Word"—and in this study of the "book of beginnings" special attention is given to the centrality of Christ as the Word of creation. Ten lessons explore truths in Genesis 1-17. **5419764**

Drinking from the Living Well: Studies in John 1-11—by Doris W. Greig
In John's Gospel we are shown that since no one can see God, Christ came to reveal Him to us. We learn of Jesus' signs and miracles in this 12-lesson course, covering John 1-11. **5419824**

Coming in 1990:

Discovering God's Protection: Studies in Genesis 32-50

Studies in Romans 1—8, 9—16

Studies in the Gospel of John 12—21

Look for these and other Regal books at your Christian bookstore.

BRING *JOY* TO A GROUP OF FRIENDS

Meet Weekly with a *Joy of Living* Bible Study Group

WHEN WE AS CHRISTIANS come together in groups, exciting things happen. We can minister to those in need, receive help when we're in need, and most importantly, grow in our relationship with Christ.

YOU CAN EXPERIENCE that growth and fellowship by starting a *Joy of Living* Bible Study Group for yourself and a group of your friends, or by joining a group that's already meeting in your neighborhood.

Since the early '70s, the *Joy of Living* Bible Studies have been touching the lives of countless people who have been attending these evangelical, nondenominational groups in churches and homes across America. They're groups that study the Bible together, pray for each other's needs together, and grow closer to Christ together.

The *Joy of Living* program provides individual worksheets to be completed in personal, daily Bible study. Then, when the group gets together for the weekly meeting, you'll discuss your answers, pray together, and hear a brief lecture by the *Joy* teaching leader.

The following books of the Bible are covered in the *Joy of Living* Bible Studies: Genesis, Exodus, Judges, Ruth, 1 & 2 Samuel, 1 & 2 Kings, Esther, Psalms, Daniel, Jonah, Luke, John, Acts, Philippians, Colossians, 1 Thessalonians, Hebrews, 1, 2 & 3 John and Jude.

TAKE PART IN THE JOY of fellowship and Bible study. Experience the *Joy of Living.* For free samples, full information on how to start a *Joy of Living* group or a listing of groups in your area, please write to:

**Joy of Living Bible Studies
P.O. Box 1377
Oak View, CA 93022**